LURE, LORE, AND LEGENDS

OF THE MORENO VALLEY

The Moreno Valley Writers Guild

Columbine Books

LURE, LORE, AND LEGENDS

OF THE MORENO VALLEY

The authors gratefully acknowledge the assistance of the following people, in addition to those who consented to share their family photos and to be interviewed, who are listed elsewhere in the book:

- Professor Carlos Vasquez, Director, UNM Oral History Program, who conducted a workshop for our writers and offered continuing support and encouragement.

- Bill Erwin, attorney, for his legal advice.

- Sandra Miller, for photo processing.

- Guy and Marcia Wood, *Sangre de Cristo Chronicle*, for permission to use the newspaper's archival material.

- Angel Fire Chamber of Commerce and the Village of Angel Fire, for financially supporting the publication costs.

- Nadine Ashcraft, president of the Angel Fire Chamber of Commerce in 1995 and the Chamber's Board of Directors, who first suggested this project to the Moreno Valley Writers Guild.

- Mary Cimarolli-Robottom, John Howard, Jo Bynum, Connie Shelton, and Elaine Jarzen for copy editing and proof-reading.

- Jack Urban, for coordinating the entire project and serving as editor for the original edition.

- Connie Shelton, whose company Columbine Publishing Group provided typesetting, layout, and production.

- Brenda Crank and Joe Haukebo, Hawk Publications, for the first edition's cover artwork.

- Columbine Books for the third edition's cover artwork.

- Agnes Arko Gibson and Donna Blades Parker for their invaluable assistance in typing, compiling, and organizing material for the 2021 third edition.

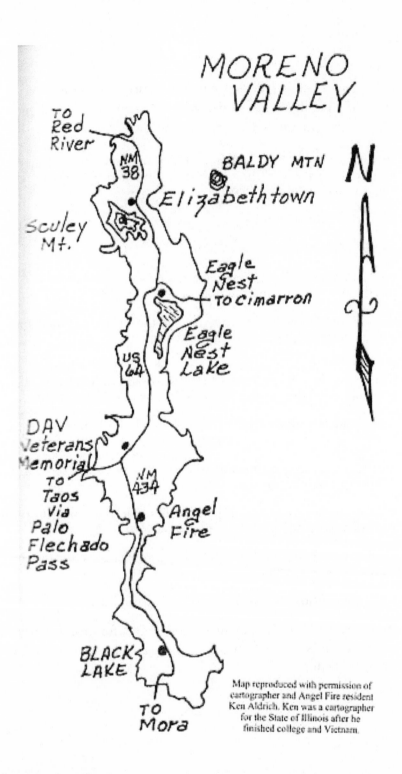

MORENO VALLEY

TO Red River

NM 38

BALDY MTN

Elizabethtown

Sculey Mt.

Eagle Nest
TO Cimarron

Eagle Nest Lake

US 64

DAV Veterans Memorial
TO Taos via Palo Flechado Pass

NM 434

Angel Fire

BLACK LAKE

TO Mora

N

Map reproduced with permission of
cartographer and Angel Fire resident
Ken Aldrich. Ken was a cartographer
for the State of Illinois after he
finished college and Vietnam.

Preface (or: How this book came to be)

Late one afternoon in the summer of 1995, my telephone rang. I picked it up, with no idea what an important turn the Moreno Valley Writers Guild would take as a result. On the line was Nadine Ashcraft, president of the Angel Fire Chamber of Commerce. In response to numerous requests by visitors to our valley, the Chamber was asking whether the Writers Guild would be willing to take on the project of writing the history of Angel Fire.

With only the vaguest notion of the daunting task ahead, I took the idea to the next membership meeting. We had just finished publishing our third anthology of the members' creative work and everyone felt ready to take on something new. The members grabbed the idea of the history book project with great enthusiasm.

The book grew from a history of Angel Fire to a history of the entire Moreno Valley, encompassing as much as possible from Elizabethtown to Black Lake. We discussed the means of collecting the data we would need and realized that there was very little written history of our area. We also realized that many of our "old time" residents were now in their 80s and 90s and that recording their stories should be of utmost importance. We knew what we wanted to do but were unsure exactly how to go about it. Enter Professor Carlos Vasquez, Director of the UNM Oral History Program.

Dr. Vasquez very generously came to Angel Fire and gave an all-day seminar on the techniques of preserving oral histories and the means of archiving the stories for future generations. Our members hit the valley, tape recorders in hand, intent on capturing as many memories as possible. The *Sangre de Cristo Chronicle* published our plea for valley residents to come forward and be included by talking to us. And talk to us, they did.

Our publishing schedule was an ambitious one, but local residents came through with material and the writers worked vigorously. Everyone was most generous - from the many residents who loaned irreplaceable family photos, to the Chamber of Commerce and Village of Angel Fire who each helped with publication costs. The research led our writers through several states and into a variety of dusty archives. In spring of 1997, at last the writing was done. The resulting book was quite successful locally, going into several printings.

Over time, the book went out of print and the Moreno Valley Writers Guild disbanded. The original manuscript files were nowhere to be found, and the original historic photos were no longer available for a new edition. In mid-2021, I was approached once again about the possibility of bringing the book back for the many newer residents and visitors to our lovely area. Donna Blades Parker and Agnes Arko Gibson eagerly volunteered to take on the challenging task of typing the text and scanning the old photos for another printing. Columbine Books, the original publisher, commissioned a new cover design, and a thorough review was conducted and new material added by third- and fourth-generation Valley residents. Where we knew historical information to have been incorrect, we updated a few things. Otherwise, these stories are exactly as told to the writers more than 25 years ago. Certain organizations and businesses have come and gone; officers and owners of those organizations have changed over time. As you read, do keep in mind that this is an oral history, with all the rich traditions of stories remembered by those who were there.

Congratulations to all involved, for this is truly a community effort. We hope you will enjoy seeing your family names in print and we hope you will share this, *your* book, with friends and relatives everywhere. We dedicate this book to all of you.

Connie Shelton, past-President
Moreno Valley Writers Guild
November, 2021

Table of Contents

Foreword

New Mexico has experienced (or suffered) several cycles of discovery. The Pueblo peoples, descendants of those noble Anasazi who had the wisdom to abandon large population centers when their exhausted lands threatened extinction, discovered they could survive and recreate their culture, stringing a necklace of villages along the Rio Grande; the fierce Apache and Navajo warriors who plied their skills as horsemen discovered a place in which they could build permanent and stable communities; the Spanish "conquistadores" discovered not fabulous wealth in precious metals, but a place where they built one of their most successful and long-lived colonizing efforts; the aggressive and enterprising Americans whose manifest destiny called for an empire on two coasts discovered, in time, that New Mexico was more than a place, in the way and on the way to somewhere else; the "lungers" discovered a climate which could cure what science and medicine could not; the migrant seasonal tourists discovered that their places of recreation were replete with rich and interesting history still to be unearthed.

Each wave of "discoverers" saw something in this harsh but beautiful land that defined for them a sense of place. And each wave has inspired a deeper search into the historical roots of this place. For despite its rich recorded history, New Mexico still has many places about which little is known or has been written. A case in point is the beautiful Moreno Valley in northern New Mexico. Popularly known for its excellent winter leisure and sports facilities, it also has a fascinating history of adventure, of industriousness, of chicanery, and of violence. The Moreno Valley Writers Guild has done an excellent job, under the leadership of Jack Urban, in uncovering the myriad stories which comprise the rich historical tapestry of the region. They have begun an enterprise others are sure to join.

In employing the oral history interview to augment their archival research, the writers have drawn on the fecundity, and the foibles, of human memory and in doing so have united a set of stories which offer glimpses and insights into a history which even those whose families have lived in the state for generations, have never heard. If there are still gaping holes in the tapestry, it is because of the unwillingness of some to share their stories, and not for the lack of effort or due to the oversight of the Writers Guild.

It was an honor to play even a minor role in introducing these hardy souls to the arduous but fulfilling work of incorporating oral testimony into historical research. They applied their writer's sensibility and its attendant demand for perfection to a task few have attempted before. Their product speaks for itself. It is a labor of love and literary courage. It is a gift given back to a region which has brought them so much joy and pleasure. What more can one ask of someone who discovers that a sense of place demands a sense of curiosity and an acknowledgement of a debt owed those who came before and who might have been relegated to oblivion by the oversight of professional historians had they not taken pen and microphone in hand?

Carlos Vasquez
The University of New Mexico
February 12, 1997

The Moreno Valley and the Colfax County War

By Jack C. Urban

Northern New Mexico's Moreno Valley is a nineteen-mile strip of land nestled among the Sangre de Cristo Mountains, twenty miles east of Taos. It takes its name from the Moreno River, meaning "dark," which flows north to south into Eagle Nest Lake. The Valley's size is not significant, but its history is tumultuous and fascinating.

Spanish explorers and Native American tribes traveled the land as a gateway to the Great Plains. Since 1541, the Spaniards were looking for gold while mapping and naming their newly acquired territory, unaware that the Moreno Valley eventually would reveal the largest deposit in New Mexico. Native Americans from Taos Pueblo, as well as the Moache Utes and Jicarilla Apaches, were establishing sacred shrines, erecting villages or camps, grazing their animals, hunting for elk and deer and moving through the Cimarron Canyon into the plains, where buffalo were abundant.

This common land concept changed in 1841. Charles Beaubien, a Canadian-born resident of Taos who became a Mexican citizen, applied to the governor in Santa Fe for a land grant. He chose as his partner, Guadalupe Miranda, an influential public servant who happened to be the governor's secretary. The boundaries of the proposed grant were described by visual landmarks. There was no survey in our understanding of the term. What they applied for was an amount of land encompassing acreage extending through north central New Mexico into what is now southern Colorado. No previous land grant application had requested such a vast territory.

Before any effective opposition could be mounted, Governor Manuel Armijo approved the grant, three days after the application was submitted. Now known as the Beaubien-Miranda Grant, it was controversial from the beginning. Leading the opposition was the parish priest of Taos, Antonio Jose Martinez, who actively championed the communal property rights of

13

Native American and Hispanic settlers. Martinez protested that the grant was invalid because it far exceeded the maximum allowed, which in this case was 92,000 acres. Little did he know how right he was. When a survey was eventually made, some 35 years later, the grant would encompass 1,714,764 acres!

When Armijo left office, Martinez temporarily succeeded in getting the grant rescinded. However, the new governor was unpopular, having proposed new taxes, and a civil disturbance erupted. Armijo was instrumental in restoring peace and Mexico City rewarded him with another term as governor. This resilient politician restored the legal status of the Beaubien-Miranda Grant. It was strongly suspected, but never proven, that Armijo was a silent partner in the enterprise, having secret ownership of one-third of the vast acreage which included the Moreno Valley.

The decision of an American frontiersman to settle down in Taos and find a bride was the next important event which would influence the land grant and the Moreno Valley. Lucien Bonaparte Maxwell, related to the famous Menard family of Illinois, married one of Charles Beaubien's daughters. As a wedding gift his father-in-law gave him 15,000 acres of grant land. It seemed at the time that this would be the extent of Maxwell's participation. The heir to Beaubien's estate was his son, Narciso.

The outcome of the 1846 Mexican American War and the subsequent rebellion in Taos a year later changed the status quo. Narciso was killed in the Taos uprising. Beaubien, having lost his only son, chose Maxwell as his successor and heir. After Beaubien's death in 1864, Maxwell purchased the shares owned by other family members as well as those owned by his father-in-law's partners. He became the sole owner of the largest privately owned piece of property in the entire United States.

In 1860, an act of the U.S. Congress declared the boundaries of the land grant to be valid. Congress quoted verbatim the landmarks described in the original 1841 grant application. Future developments would ignore or lose sight of this important decision.

Maxwell established the towns of Rayado and Cimarron. The Moreno Valley served as the connecting link between the grant and Taos. Historians are fond of calling Maxwell's property a "baronial empire." His was a one-man rule with growth managed by his own decisions. He had the reputation of being a generous man and a kind host to strangers. He had the government contract to feed the native tribes who continued to live in the Sangre de Cristo foothills. His empire was protected by the proximity of Fort Union, a day's ride from Cimarron. He welcomed the wagon trains taking the Northern Route of the Santa Fe Trail. He encouraged pioneers like Manley Chase and John Dawson to buy land at low prices and generous terms. All this activity was east of the Moreno Valley, good for grazing cattle but little more.

Then came 1866 and the discovery of gold on Baldy Mountain in the northern Moreno Valley. Elizabethtown was founded in the spring of 1867 and within a year's time had a population approaching 7,000. In numbers alone, what was once fallow land was approaching the population of Santa Fe. Maxwell's dream of managed and controlled growth, determined by him alone, was abruptly shattered.

He was not totally unprepared for this dramatic change of events, aware that his grant had rich mineral deposits although he did not explore its extent himself. He knew the property he sold to John Dawson was rich in coal, but neither man realized at the time the bonanza which would develop. Gold was another matter. The boom could last for a few years or extend into decades. Maxwell took two courses of action. He built his own mining operation on Baldy Mountain and also established lease agreements with the new arrivals, showing his characteristic generosity.

But as is often the course of human nature, there were those who felt no need to legitimize their presence on Maxwell's property. Maxwell himself was not inclined to take drastic action against the squatters.

When the Moreno Valley was thrust from obscurity into prominence, the federal government took a second look at the validity of the land grant itself. A survey had never been made. Boundaries were obscure. Two federal departments were debating the grant's legal status: The Federal Surveyors Office and the Department of the Interior. The size of the grant, far exceeding the maximum allowed by Spanish-Mexican law, had once again surfaced as an issue. Perhaps the government would declare the grant to be public domain, the squatters reasoned, available for prospecting or homesteading. So why settle with Maxwell? The Moreno Valley was caught in the middle of this controversy and the convulsions which followed.

Without making his reasons known, Maxwell made a fateful decision in 1870. He would sell the grant, leaving for himself his two-story mansion in Cimarron and the adjacent 1200 acres. He optioned the property to three Colorado businessmen who had strong financial and political ties in Washington D.C. and Europe. This was an era when foreign investors were buying large tracts in the western United States, anticipating huge profits from westward immigration. They produced colorful and sometimes exaggerated brochures illustrating the glories of their property. One brochure produced for the Maxwell Land Grant shows a Mississippi-style steamboat paddling down the Cimarron River!

Within a year, the Colorado group sold the grant to British investors who in turn sold to a Dutch consortium in Amsterdam. Maxwell's share of the profits was $650,000 or about $13 million in 1990s money. He bought the abandoned Fort Sumner and Bosque Redondo property in east central New Mexico where he lived until his death in 1875.

When the gold-producing Moreno Valley and the rest of the grant acreage was sold to foreign investors, they were told they had "a perfectly valid title" to the property based on the 1860 Act of Congress. What they purchased was a quagmire of controversy which would come to be known as the Colfax County War.

Why was the grant called "Colfax" County? Logic would tell us that "Maxwell" would have been more appropriate. It is a quirk of history that a now obscure politician achieved that honor. Schuyler Colfax, as newly elected Vice President of the United States, visited northern New Mexico and Colorado shortly before the beginning of Ulysses S. Grant's first administration. To curry favor and honor their distinguished guest, the citizens of Elizabethtown petitioned the Territorial Legislature to create a county named after the new Vice President. On January 25, 1869, the petition was approved. At the time, the new county included all Maxwell Grant property (excepting the 265,000 acres in southern Colorado) plus additional land extending to the Texas-Oklahoma border.

The Elizabethtown politicians had an agenda. They promptly made sure that their town would become the first county seat, giving them legal jurisdiction over this vast section of northern New Mexico. In two years, the Moreno Valley had emerged from a cattle grazing enclave into the most important political and population center north of Santa Fe. It was even proposed that Elizabethtown replace Santa Fe as the state capital! Nothing came of this ambitious idea.

The first task of the newly formed Maxwell Land Company was to sort out who among the settlers had lease or sales agreements with Maxwell and who were squatters. At first, polite notices were sent to those who were identified as squatters. They refused to budge. The matter was then turned over to State Attorney General Thomas B. Catron, to prepare eviction notices. Catron was controversial because of friendship and business ties with Stephen Elkins, the president of the land company board of directors. The result was a riot breaking out in Elizabethtown only a few months after the foreign investors took control. It was so serious that Elkins petitioned the governor to send soldiers to restore order. This action galvanized the anti-grant forces who were now even more determined to maintain their position.

The Moreno Valley was the center of discontent for two years. Then the eye of the storm moved north. In 1872, the county seat with all its judicial and record keeping privileges was transferred to Cimarron. This also happened to be the headquarters of the land grant company. More eviction notices were served but these were ignored.

Hoping to break the impasse, the company elected a young, ambitious, and highly skilled civil engineer as its vice-president and chief operating officer, William Raymond Morley, who took a leave of absence as chief construction engineer for the Santa Fe Railroad. The railroad was only six years away from entering New Mexico. He was aware that the grant controlled the key right-of-way over Raton Pass, connecting the territory with southern Colorado. His new position was unenviable, but it would strengthen the relationship between the railroad and the grant company.

Aware of the gridlock between the pro and anti-grant factions, Morley sent word to his native Iowa requesting his friend Frank W. Springer come to Cimarron and help sort out the problem. Morley made an excellent choice. Springer was an attorney of brilliant intellect who could argue complicated cases with ease and clarity. He was even tempered, analytical and honest. He would become one of the most respected of the territorial pioneers. Colfax County would be his home well into the 20th century. The

17

CS Ranch which he owned in partnership with his brother Charles is still owned and operated by his descendants. Part of the ranch is in the Moreno Valley.

Morley's efforts to bring peace were further complicated in 1874. The Federal Department of Interior, ignoring the 1860 Act of Congress, declared the land grant to be public domain, entrenching the anti-grant position. To make matters worse, the land grant company was nearing bankruptcy. Even the payment of property taxes was a burden. A third complication came from the board of directors itself.

There was talk in Santa Fe that prominent Republican men had formed a secret coalition designed to control public offices, especially the judiciary. The public called the shadowy group "The Santa Fe Ring," accusing it of all sorts of nefarious deeds. In Territorial New Mexico effective libel laws were almost non-existent. Rumor and fact became intermingled. Reputations were defended by denial or violence. It is difficult for historians to sift through the accusations made about the Ring and determine their validity. The Ring was not about to issue denials and expose its existence and agenda. What is said in the following paragraphs reflects only the prevailing attitude at the time.

Widely suspected as members of the Ring were men associated with the Maxwell Land Company's board of directors: Stephen Elkins, Dr. Robert Longwill, and Thomas B. Catron who no longer held his position as state attorney general. Morley and Springer became suspicious of possible hidden motives. This would emerge when the Maxwell Company defaulted on its property tax obligation. A public auction was declared, with an associate of Thomas Catron buying the grant for $16,479 in back taxes, intending to sell it to Catron for $20,000. The associate was Melvin W. Mills, an attorney also suspected as a Ring member. Fortunately for the Maxwell Company there remained a grace period. When the Catron plan was exposed, the Dutch owners raised enough money to redeem the property.

Morley and Springer began a newspaper, *The Cimarron News and Press*, which regularly criticized the Santa Fe Ring and its objectives. Both would later be marked for assassination, with the Ring suspected of plotting the scheme.

These ingredients of intrigue and unrest reached the explosion stage in September 1875 with the murder of Reverend Franklin J. Tolby. The young Methodist minister and his wife moved to Cimarron in January of the previous year, with the Moreno Valley as part of his ministry. The Anglo Protestant community was proud to have its first resident pastor. Mild mannered in appearance, he was an outspoken social activist unafraid to speak out in favor of the anti-grant settlers. He publicly criticized Judge Joseph Palen and the grand jury for not indicting a local gunman, Pancho Griego, who had killed two soldiers in a gambling quarrel. Griego had the reputation of being a local enforcer for the Santa Fe Ring. Judge Palen was widely suspected as being a member of the Ring's inner circle. The outspoken Tolby declared that he would "write up the judge so the 200,000 readers would see his record." Two months before Tolby's murder a letter appeared in the *New York Sun* exposing the Santa Fe Ring and naming Palen, Elkins, and Catron as key members. The letter was unsigned. It was later discovered that a certain Simeon H. Newman had written the letter, but this was not known at the time.

On Monday, September 14th, Tolby was returning through the Cimarron Canyon after conducting Sunday services in the Moreno Valley. Two days later his body was found shot two times in the back, all his belongings intact and his horse neatly tied to a nearby tree. The county was enraged. Tolby, the activist hero, became a martyr for the anti-grant cause. Anyone connected with the Santa Fe Ring was suspect.

There was irony in Tolby's murder. Those who planned his assassination thought his death would frighten or silence opposition. What they experienced was a backlash which would plunge the county into a vigilante justice mentality for the next twelve years: The Colfax County War.

Emerging from the indignation over Tolby's murder was a new leader, the Rev. Oscar P. McMains. He had been the Rev. Tolby's part-time assistant, supporting himself as a printer at Morley and Springer's newspaper. A small man with a booming voice, contemporaries called him an orator of persuasive ability. Tolby's outspokenness would pale compared to McMains' thundering and tenacious struggle on behalf of the anti-grant settlers.

The question in everyone's mind was why Tolby's body had been discovered two days after the killing when on the Monday of the shooting there was a mail delivery through the Canyon with Tolby's horse in plain sight and the body lying nearby. McMains and his newly formed vigilante group confronted the mail contractor, Florencio Donoghue, who had suspected ties with the Santa Fe Ring. The frightened Donoghue said he had hired a man named Cruz Vega to deliver the mail that day. Vega, it was learned, was hired only for this one occasion. Donoghue told the mob that Vega was staying at a ranch in the Moreno Valley.

Wearing hoods, the vigilantes rode the 30 miles to the Valley, captured Vega, tied him to a tree in a hanging position and tortured him until he confessed. Vega shouted his innocence but implicated a certain Manuel Cardenas who he said was also hired by Donoghue to kill Tolby. Cardenas, he said, did the actual killing. The mob was now out of control and Vega was hanged.

Cardenas was arrested by the legal authorities and insisted that Vega had done the shooting. More damaging, he implicated two suspected members of the Santa Fe Ring: Dr. Robert Longwill and attorney Melvin Mills. The hearing lasted into the evening with Cardenas changing his story, denying any connection with the Tolby murder. As he was being led from the courtroom to the jail, an assassin shot him dead and escaped into the darkness.

During all these events Melvin Mills was in Colorado and, upon hearing of the Cardenas accusation, voluntarily returned to Cimarron. He was threatened by mob violence but stood his ground, requesting a court hearing. Frank Springer, no friend of the Ring, ably defended him. The Cardenas charge was dismissed for lack of evidence. Mills, however, was dogged by the accusation the rest of his life.

When Robert Longwill heard of the Cardenas testimony, he hastily left town pursued by a posse led by famed gunman, Clay Allison. Allison was a local rancher whose hot temper, hard drinking lifestyle, vigilante justice mentality, and quick gun gave him notoriety as far away as Dodge City. Three days after the hanging of Vega, he was stalked by Pancho Griego who had vowed to avenge his friend Vega's death. Griego suspected that Allison was one of the hooded vigilantes. The two men met at the St.

James Hotel in Cimarron. Owner Henry Lambert poured each a drink, hoping to cool things down. Griego took off his hat, pretending to fan himself, while reaching for his gun. Allison spotted the ruse and shot him dead. The killing was ruled self-defense.

Longwill made it to his home, telling his wife that if anyone came in pursuit to tell them he was suffering from cholera. Changing horses, he rode full speed to safety in Santa Fe. He was never heard from again, reinforcing in the public mind his complicity in Tolby's murder.

The Rev. McMains was charged with inciting the mob violence that led to Vega's hanging. He was defended by Frank Springer. The jury declared him guilty of "a felony in the fifth degree," fining him $300. It was tantamount to acquittal.

Four months after Tolby's murder, the state legislature transferred all judicial powers in Colfax County to Taos County. To stifle opposition, Governor Samuel Axtell signed the bill which was passed on the last day of the legislative session. The county was again in an uproar.

Springer, Morley, Allison, and business leader Henry M. Porter invited the governor to come to Cimarron to show him that conditions had settled down, hoping to convince him that judicial power should be restored to Colfax County. Some considered the governor to be a tool of the Santa Fe Ring, but the four community leaders felt obliged to present their case.

There now developed a chain of events worthy of the most imaginative fiction writer. Benjamin Stevens, the District Attorney for the 2nd Judicial District at Las Vegas, was the intermediary between the governor and the county leaders. What Morley, Springer, Allison, and Porter didn't know was that they would be marked for assassination. Allison, with his unpredictable and volatile nature, was the main target. In March 1876, Stevens met with Morley, saying the governor would come to Cimarron, and arranged a specific day for the meeting on one condition: the meeting was to be private with no public announcement and no crowd present. Stevens then went to Ft. Union and returned to Cimarron with a company of black soldiers known in history as the famed "Buffalo Soldiers" of the Ninth Cavalry.

Their selection was premeditated. Allison, the ex-Confederate soldier, was known to be a Yankee hater with animosity toward blacks. It was hoped that the hot-tempered Allison would become confrontational, providing an excuse to kill him. Stevens told the committee of four that the governor would arrive by coach the following Saturday.

Axtell had no intention of coming. Instead, he wrote a letter to Stevens, now known in history as the infamous "Dear Ben" letter, advising Stevens, "Do not hesitate at extreme measures. Your honor is at stake now and a failure is fatal."

The letter was placed in a trunk marked for Stevens and sent by stagecoach to Cimarron. The trunk was stolen and somehow the letter came into the possession of Frank Springer. The details of this chain of events remain a mystery. What is known is that Thomas Catron placed an ad in the Las Vegas newspaper offering a substantial reward for the return of the trunk. The letter today resides in the archives of the CS Ranch.

Springer informed the others and the plot failed. The next day, Springer wrote to the governor about the contents of the letter which was written in pencil on plain paper with no official letterhead. Axtell lamely replied that the letter must have been a forgery. A month later Ben Stevens died of natural causes. However, the captain of the Buffalo Soldier company would later confirm that an assassination plot was planned, with Allison the main target. In 1878, President Rutherford B. Hayes removed Axtell from office, replacing him with the Civil War hero Lew Wallace, who later became famous as the author of *Ben Hur*.

Morley resigned from the board of directors of the company, now known as the Maxwell Land Grant and Railway Company. He returned as chief construction engineer for the Santa Fe Railroad as it turned south from La Junta, Colorado, poised to enter New Mexico. Henry M. Porter continued his banking and mercantile businesses but would later base his operations in Denver. Clay Allison settled with the land grant company, sold his ranch, and moved to Pecos, Texas. Frank Springer remained a key figure in the county and achieved even greater respect in the legal and ranching professions. He would also become a world-famous paleontologist.

All these violent events did not settle the basic question about the grant—private property or public domain? In 1882 the federal government finally presented a case challenging the validity of the grant. It filed a bill in the U.S. District Court in Colorado alleging the grant "to be falsely, fraudulently and deceitfully surveyed." Mainly at issue were the 265,000 land grant acres in Colorado. The federal government had planned to conduct its own survey but had not done so. In 1877 the Maxwell Land Grant and Railway Company decided to conduct a private survey, giving the contract to John Elkins, the brother of one of the company's board of directors. Elkins was a competent surveyor but his relationship with the board called into question his objectivity.

Frank Springer had two roles in the case. As a member of the board, he was a defendant. As chief legal counsel for the company, he defended the grant's interests. The government case was based upon the appearance of wrongdoing, but as testimony was presented, its case began to unravel. Springer called as witnesses colorful mountaineers such as Calvin Jones and "Uncle Dick" Wootton who were familiar with the original boundary markings dating back to the days of Mexican rule. Elkins' survey books were carefully examined and found to be basically accurate. The district court ruled in favor of the Maxwell Land Grant and Railway Company. Embarrassed federal officials then appealed the case to the United States Supreme Court. Five years later, as final arbiter in the matter, the Court would decide the fate of the land grant. The "perfectly valid title" had one more legal hurdle to overcome.

In the meantime, the Rev. Oscar P. McMains was not idle. He traveled to Washington to lobby for squatters' rights. He began a newspaper, *The Raton Comet,* supporting the anti-grant position. When his own property was placed on public auction by the land grant company, his supporters showed up with shotguns, daring anyone to make a bid. No one did.

In 1885 more violence broke out. The land grant company was conducting an aggressive campaign supported by court orders to remove settlers whose property was not sanctioned by the company. They hired 35 enforcers led by James Masterson, brother of the famous "Bat" Masterson. The company prevailed upon the governor to give the enforcers militia status, a stamp of official approval. *The Raton Comet* exposed the plan as organized by "the vampires and land grant pirates of New Mexico."

Six years earlier, the railroad had created the town of Raton, which was fast becoming the most important population center in the county. A committee of Raton citizens went to Santa Fe and successfully convinced the governor that Masterson's so-called militiamen were all "gunmen, killers, thugs, and bums from places outside New Mexico." Masterson's answer to this turn of events was to pistol whip one of the Raton committee members and throw his body in the gutter. Despite the governor's rescinding of official sanction, the enforcers were not about to disband.

Under the leadership of George Curry, later Territorial Governor of New Mexico, 600 county citizens met at the Raton Rink to determine a course of action. They purchased all the guns and ammunition available in Raton. One hundred fifty men patrolled the streets to keep order. Oscar McMains made sure all the saloons were closed. The plan was to take Masterson and his men into custody, lead them to the Colorado border and warn them never to return to New Mexico. The show of force succeeded. Masterson and his men meekly left the state.

But Curry's orderly solution to one problem was shattered five days later in the town of Springer, which by then had replaced Cimarron as the county seat. A certain John Dodds from Crow Creek Ranch came to Springer to sell and buy supplies. He proceeded to get drunk, shooting up the town and fighting with the constable. It didn't mean much at the time, but Constable Carter and his deputy were pro-grant enforcers. Dodds happened to belong to the anti-grant faction. The rancher was arrested, fined, and released. That should have concluded the matter. But Constable Carter, unhappy with the judge's verdict, decided to re-arrest Dodds on a charge of assault and battery, himself being the victim. Dodds eluded Carter and his deputy, Jesse Lee, riding back to Springer and telegraphing Raton for help.

The incident then escalated into a shootout with pro and anti-grant overtones. Five men from Raton, including the younger brother of George Curry, rode to Springer to help Dodds, who by this time had been recaptured and jailed. Two of the five decided to approach the jail unarmed, hoping to resolve the matter peacefully. As they approached, Deputy Lee opened fire, killing them both. Nineteen-year-old John Curry returned fire and was mortally wounded. He would later die in the arms of his older brother.

The telegraph reported to Raton what had happened. George Curry and 40 men rushed to Springer, took over the telegraph office and proceeded to lay siege around the jail complex. Melvin Mills was in town at the time and rode to Wagon Mound, telegraphing the governor of these developments. Twenty soldiers and two officers from Ft. Union boarded a special train at Watrous, some 40 miles from Springer, arriving before more violence occurred.

The vigilantes and the army officers held a meeting resulting in the arrest of Deputy Lee for killing unarmed men. Curry was also arrested for holding the town hostage. Lee was transferred to Taos but never brought to trial. After three weeks in jail, Curry finally posted a $5,000 bond. Special prosecutor Thomas B. Catron, unwelcome in the county for many reasons, received death threats. The Curry matter was dropped. John Dodds' re-arrest was rescinded. His routine decision to sell corn in Springer had resulted in three deaths, a vigilante takeover of the town and a military intervention. Lucien Maxwell's quiet empire had now seen fifteen years of tinderbox turmoil.

Throughout this contentious time, the anti-grant settlers had ignored the 1860 Act of Congress declaring the grant to be private property. The federal bureaucracy contributed to their position by resurrecting earlier objections that the grant exceeded the maximum allowed under Spanish-Mexican law and that its boundary markings were suspect. Both parties pinned their hopes on the Supreme Court reversing the Colorado decision and dismissing the 1860 Act of Congress.

Aware of the protracted dispute since 1870, the Supreme Court gave priority to the hearing of this case. Argument was scheduled to begin March 8, 1887. Representing the Maxwell Land Grant and Railway Company was Frank W. Springer. After four days of oral argument and 900 pages of testimony, the court handed down its decision five weeks later. The 1860 Act of Congress became the focus of their ruling. The court concluded: "We are entirely satisfied that the Grant, as confirmed by the action of Congress, is a valid grant, that the survey and the patent issued upon it are entirely free from any fraud."

For Frank Springer this was the high point of his legal career. For Oscar McMains and the anti-grant settlers it dashed any hope of legal recourse. McMains would move to Colorado. Most of the settlers who had no legal status would move elsewhere or come to terms with the company.

Pockets of resistance would remain. Hispanic families who had settled near Rayado, generations before, were finally evicted in 1894. Richard Russell defended what he thought to be homesteading rights and was killed in an 1888 shootout with the company enforcers near his ranch in Stonewall, Colorado. His wife, the famous pioneer chronicler Marian Sloan Russell, produced homestead papers but the court eventually ruled against her.

What began in the Moreno Valley with the discovery of gold had mushroomed into a 17-year struggle enveloping two states. As the valley emerged into the 20th century the turmoil of past decades was replaced by a quieter existence. Elizabethtown continued to produce some gold but was no longer a bustling boom town populated by thousands. Ranchers and farmers went about their business on land once traveled by vigilante mobs. Unheralded in this story are the pioneer families who toiled throughout those tumultuous years creating a stability into which our modern era would emerge.

Today the Moreno Valley is best known for its resort and recreational attractions. We call it a part of "The Enchanted Circle." In the chapters which follow our writers tell of the towns the Valley created, featuring interviews with pioneer families. Their personal memories bring a human touch to the historical events which make the Moreno Valley what it is today.

This book is by no means definitive: other stories are to be told. Our goal is to put in writing a beginning process to encourage others to add to the Lure, Lore, and Legends of the Moreno Valley.

* * *

In the 1990s Jack C. Urban devoted his full time to the research and study of northern New Mexico history. He published a vintage style newspaper celebrating the 175th anniversary of the Santa Fe Trail and was a frequent contributor to Hawk Publications. His business, Posters from Angel Fire, combined vintage photos with text describing New Mexico history.

The Geology of the Moreno Valley

By Scott Lysinger

"Sangre de Cristo Mountains, Taos Plateau, Rio Grande Gorge—the geology of north-central New Mexico is as diverse and spectacular as any place on Earth." *—The Enchanted Circle Loop Drive from Taos.*

The Moreno Valley originated about 300 million years ago in an area on the earth's surface about 2,500 miles south of its present location. It was in a shallow marine basin that sand and clay of Pennsylvanian age was deposited via erosion and run-off from adjacent headlands.

Ecologists have determined that the life forms indigenous to the strata were compatible with a warm equatorial environment. These sediments formed sandstones, shales, and limestones that are visible today in outcrops and road cuts, notably along U.S. Highway 64 between Taos and the base of Palo Flechado Pass.

Time passed—260 million years—and the valley, now a part of the North American Continental Plate, drifted northward, a few centimeters a year, to its present geographical location in north central New Mexico.

Concurrently, intense Rocky Mountain structural movements uplifted the Taos Range and thus set the western wall of the future Moreno Valley. At that time, an eastward view from that location would display a Piedmont-type plain with ancestral streams carrying sediments downslope to the prairies of Oklahoma and Texas. This material formed water reserves which would later be important to the agriculture of that region. Large mammals roamed the grasslands.

The final framing event of the valley occurred when the Cimarron Range was uplifted on the east side about 30 million years ago. Opposing high-angle faults separated the ranges with a central down-dropped Graben block.

Spectacular volcanics, along the length and breadth of the Cimarron

Range, intruded the strata and poured lava down the slopes. Molten globs ejected high in the air, solidified as volcanic bombs, and were dropped in one area on what is now the Philmont Scout Ranch. The lava flows and faulting effectively dammed up all avenues of water drainage from the valley. Lakes and marshes covered the valley floor for several million years until erosion breached the barriers on Cimarron Creek and Coyote Creek, thus re-establishing run-off to the east and south.

Today the Black Lakes of far southwestern Colfax County are the only remaining vestiges of the time when Moreno Valley was Moreno Lake.

In 1918, the CS Ranch restored one of nature's better ideas by building a dam, advanced in design and foresight, across Cimarron Canyon impounding beautiful Eagle Nest Lake.

In 1990, geologists from over the world gathered for a three-day field conference in the southern Sangre de Cristo Mountains. Their objective was to study the geological history of the region. A guidebook was prepared for the meeting by the New Mexico Geological Society, *Tectonic Development of the Southern Sangre de Cristo Mountains, New Mexico*. It contains a road log with mileage to points of interest and numerous dissertations by experts on the physical and historical attractions in the area.

This publication, along with another, *The Enchanted Circle, Loop Drives from Taos*, is available from The New Mexico Bureau of Mines and Minerals, Socorro, NM 87801. The Loop Drives book is also available at regional bookstores.

* * *

Angel Fire resident Scott Lysinger spent a lifetime in geology and he served as an oil industry consultant for petroleum exploration. In 1979 Scott and his wife Rose built a vacation home in Black Lake, and Angel Fire became their full-time home for a number of years beginning in 1989.

Native Americans in the Moreno Valley

By Claude McDonald and Fran Pallesen

"Native Americans Discovered America." So reads the bumper sticker on the late model Dodge Ram. That is a profound reminder to all. It follows that Native Americans discovered this beautiful Moreno (Dark) Valley.

Members of several tribes enjoyed the summer coolness of the Moreno Valley between the Sangre de Cristo (Blood of Christ) Mountains on the west and Cimarron Mountain Range on the east, even as we enjoy it today.

We are informed that some of the Native Americans from the Taos Pueblo would pitch their wigwams along the streams in the valley as soon as the winter snows began to melt and remain until the aspen turned to gold. Although the growing season in the Moreno Valley was short, they were able to plant and harvest squash and tubers such as carrots and potatoes. Small game from the mountains provided some meat, however, the bulk of the meat came from buffalo hunted on the plains surrounding the mountain ranges. The winters were too severe for them to remain in the mountain's valley, so they retreated to their multi-storied adobe-constructed pueblos in Taos for the cold months.

The Taos Pueblo inhabitants influenced the Plains Indians as early as 1200 A.D., sharing with them knowledge of farming and crafts, particularly pottery making. From this beginning, the Taos Pueblo commanded a position as a major Native American trading center. From the 13th to the latter part of the 19th centuries, Apaches, Comanches, Kiowas, Utes, and several other tribes made their journey from the plains into Taos.

Two routes were prevalent from the eastern plains into the main center of trading at Taos Pueblo. Both of these thoroughfares passed through the Moreno Valley. The most heavily traveled was the path coming from the east through present-day Cimarron, Ute Park and Eagle Nest. Less traveled was the southern route through present-day Mora, Guadalupita,

Coyote State Park, Black Lake and Angel Fire. One of the reasons for this being less popular was that the Picuris and Pecos Pueblos began to rival Taos for trade by the latter part of the 16th century.

It is important to understand that the Pueblo Indians had an edge on the Plains Indians in developing crafts. Once they learned the skill of cultivating and growing corn, these Native Americans, who lived originally in the cliffs and subsequently in the multi-storied adobe dwellings, enjoyed a measure of release, with freedom to engage in activities other than providing food for subsistence.

On the other hand, the Plains Indians were forced to continue their nomadic style of life following the buffalo herds. They had little time for anything other than eking out a bare existence. Corn became a luxury to them and was a motivating factor for some of the Apaches to establish temporary gardens. They ate the corn before it fully matured, being probably the first to introduce roasting ears to other Native Americans.

All these things were factors in establishing trade. The Moreno Valley provided the crossroads leading in and out of Taos, to the eastern plains. As two routes led into the valley, so it seems, two routes led from the valley into Taos. The most traveled was the one which modern-day Highway 64 takes over Palo Flechado Pass (meaning "tree pierced with arrows"), through Taos Canyon and into Taos. It is believed that the Flecha de Palo Apache natives who inhabited the plains just east of the mountains gave the name to Palo Flechado Pass, as they left their spare arrows in the evergreens marking the trail along the way. The less traveled route was from the valley, straight over the mountain by Blue Lake. In 1906, the United States government took over the "sacred" Blue Lake and surrounding mountain lands for a National Forest. In 1970, the government returned 48,000 acres of the mountain lands, including Blue Lake, to the Taos Pueblo. These areas are off-limits to all but members of the Taos Pueblo.

It was trade that brought prominence to the Moreno Valley from the 13th until nearly the 20th centuries. During this six-hundred-year span, the Native American was at center stage in the trade scene. The Moreno Valley merely served as the route to and from the centers in Taos, Pecos, and Picuris.

Although the Native Americans traded amongst themselves, bartering buffalo meat and hides for food staples, corn, tobacco, gold, and silver. Beginning in the latter part of the 18th century the Spanish Comancheros became increasingly a factor on the trading scene. The Spaniards' objective was primarily to purchase horses from the Plains Indians, which in turn motivated the natives to steal horses from one another. Not only did they steal livestock, but certain tribes, particularly the Apaches, engaged in a slave trade, supplying Spanish traders with enslaved Native Americans from raided villages of the Caddoan tribes. These slaves were worked in the mines and used as household servants in mid-17th-century New Mexico. This Spanish greed, coupled with the ferocity of the Apaches, began a chain of events which resulted in the Pueblo Revolt of 1680. In August of that year, the Pueblo Indians of New Mexico united and drove the Spanish out of the region. The revolt reopened the door for trade with Taos and the Plains Indians. The Spanish returned in the 1690s, and eventually the Native Americans and Spanish learned to exist in semi-harmony.

The Moreno Valley was "a way through" and a beautiful place to stop and rest. It is thought that several of the Native American tribes established their own areas of encampment and enhanced their particular place with a religious shrine. Several individuals familiar with the history of the Moreno Valley say there were nine such shrines. The "Lone Pine Tree," located approximately half-way between Eagle Nest and the blinking light at the junction of Highways 64 and 434, was the only presently identified shrine in 1997. Sadly, in the mid-2000s, the tree died and is no longer there. Another may have been at Palo Flechado Pass, and a third was undoubtedly located in the Valley of the Utes. Taking the main gravel road south from the base of the Angel Fire ski basin to the Valley of the Utes is a five-mile drive more than worth the effort.

Why do we know so little about the religious and spiritual heritage of our Native American friends? The answer is explained in the single-sheet handout provided when one visits the Taos Pueblo. A statement in their *Taos Pueblo ... A Thousand Years of Tradition* states: "Our people have a detailed oral history which is not divulged due to religious privacy."

The Native Americans in the Southwest take their religious privacy seriously. Although ninety percent of the inhabitants of Taos Pueblo follow the Catholic religion, as the above-mentioned publication notes:

"The Pueblo religion is very complex; however, there is no conflict with the Catholic church, as evidenced by the prominent presence of both church and kiva (a Pueblo Indian ceremonial structure that is usually round and partly underground) in the village."

There are a multitude of Indian legends, which many people find spiritual while seeking the "Truth." One legend tells that the area immediately above the southeast corner of the Valley of the Utes was an ancient Ute burial ground. Some spiritually sensitive individuals say they experience a powerful presence as they enter the wooded area about a third of the way up the face of the mountain. Two recent legends concerning this area have made the rounds in Angel Fire.

The first legend relates to surveying equipment going berserk when surveyors from the Coo and Van Loo Company in Phoenix, Arizona began work on plotting lots in the Valley of the Utes area. The second involved two local residents who, in the early 1980s, were hunting deer on Angel Fire Mountain one winter day. As the sun set in the west they came to the road above the Valley of the Utes, and each was startled by a vision of an Indian village with men, women and children moving in and out of wigwams.

Is there an existing force that brings about a time warp in this particular area of the Sangre de Cristos? Some reputable people claim there is a force

Dr.. Victor Westphall holding a "star stone" given to him by a Native American Marine. The stone came from the shores of Lake Superior.

of energy that arises through Wheeler Peak and descends the eastern slope into the Moreno Valley. Dr. Victor Westphall, founder and builder of the Vietnam Veterans National Memorial Chapel was even more specific. In a one-page essay entitled: "The Chapel Stucco and Aboriginal Tradition - A Sacred Element" the author explains:

"Far back in the mists of antiquity there arose a tradition among the Indians who roamed the area where the Vietnam Veterans National Memorial now stands that this was sacred ground. Even today, many visitors report sensing an unaccountable spirituality in the environs of the Memorial. This phenomenon may be more than coincidence. There may be an element shared by Indians then and visitors now. There may be a primeval line of force emanating from Wheeler Peak, the highest elevation in New Mexico, passing through the area of Blue Lake, the sacred place of the Taos Pueblo Indians, and intersecting the present location of the Memorial. Aboriginal people, with their pronounced sensitivity to natural circumstances, sensed this force. More modern humans with at least rudimentary sensitivity to nature may do the same.

"It happens that the Memorial Chapel is the outstanding visual and aesthetic element in the broad confines of the Moreno Valley. The chapel is the jewel in the crown of all it surveys from its commanding site. It also happens that technical difficulties were encountered in applying the insulation layer of the stucco with the smooth surfaces considered proper for modern building excellence. The consequences are subtle undulations in the outer face and edges of that stucco's surface. Happily, what might be considered imperfections are harmonious within themselves and the total effect is pleasing to the aesthetically attuned eye. Unwittingly, the feel of hand-applied plaster, which was necessarily the technique of ancient people, is now subtly incorporated in the chapel's finished exterior surface. This is in harmony with the spirituality of this locale as recognized by our Indian forebears. It is fitting that this feature of their building practice be incorporated in this totally modern structure. It memorably binds together the ancient and new in a stunning visual reminder that we have chosen well the location for this memorial to fallen heroes."

In a subsequent interview Dr. Westphall explained that the "primeval line of force" is called "ley lines." A Native-American Vietnam veteran, who was in the Marine Corps, told Dr. Westphall that when he stood on the parking lot above the chapel and looked toward Wheeler Peak, he saw these ley lines. He described "dancing balls," which eventually disappeared, emitting from the land. The Marine gave Westphall a "star stone" or "warrior stone," perfectly symmetrical, and about the size of a tennis ball. It is quite heavy and is probably composed of iron and copper. These stones are rare and valued by the Native Americans in northern Wisconsin as they are used in healing ceremonies.

Dr. Westphall also verified surveyors in the area had told him their instruments seemed to be affected for some unknown reason. He noted further that many visitors to the chapel tell him they sense something they can't put their finger on. "This testimony happens too many times to be coincidence," Dr. Westphall said.

Ley lines, Indian lore, time-warp phenomenon ... more fact than fiction? Who knows? But the one thing we do know for certain is, as the bumper sticker on the Dodge Ram declared, "Native Americans Discovered America." Indeed they did, and their traditions remain alive in the beautiful Moreno Valley.

* * *

Fran Pallesen first saw the beauty of the Moreno Valley in 1992. She has found the Valley a fascinating study for its history, peoples, flora, and fauna. The Pallesens, formerly from New York State and then full-time RVers, called Angel Fire their hometown for a number of years.

Claude C. McDonald was a Christian Church (Disciples of Christ) clergyman, who ministered in Santa Fe for eleven years. He and his wife, Marian, lived in Angel Fire for a number of years beginning in 1975. McDonald is the author of "There's Comfort in His Love," published by Fleming Revell.

Elizabethtown — New Mexico's 'El Dorado'

By Jack C. Urban
with contributions by
Tracey Miller and Leigh Aldrich

In the fall of 1866, a Moache Ute was apprehensive about the coming of winter. The white man's rations of beef, flour and a few blankets were a limited commodity. He wanted more supplies to ensure winter survival. But what did he have of value to trade? He thought of an outcropping of colored rocks on Baldy Mountain overlooking the Moreno Valley. Perhaps these would be of interest to the white man who was constantly seeking a treasure embedded in Mother Earth.

From the valley floor, a mile and a half above sea level, he climbed an additional 4,000 feet, collecting rocks to take to Fort Union where he knew Captain William Moore, the owner of the sutler's store. Moore had been a captain in the Calvary and proudly retained that title. If Moore found them to be of value, he would barter for additional winter supplies. The Captain instantly recognized the rocks to contain a high grade of copper ore. He not only was willing to buy them but offered the Ute more supplies if he would show him the location of the outcropping.

The Ute was pleased with the arrangement. When the location of the deposit was identified, Moore and his partner, William Kroenig, shared their discovery with three others familiar with mineral assaying: Larry Bronson, Peter Kissinger, and R.P. Kelley. Moore sent the three prospectors to the site to assay the copper find. It was now October and, with winter approaching, the work had to be done quickly. While Bronson and Kissinger were setting up camp, Kelley decided to explore one of the many gully streams flowing from the mountain. He passed his time panning the gravel and, much to his amazement, he found flakes of gold! Shouting to his companions, he called them to confirm his finding.

The three men abandoned the copper ore project as they found similar gold deposits in nearly every gulch on the west side of Baldy Mountain. A snowstorm forced them to abandon the site but, before leaving, they carved the words DISCOVERY TREE on a large pine which grew nearby.

Hurrying back to Fort Union, they reported to Moore and Kroenig what they had found. The elusive El Dorado, which had eluded the Spaniards three centuries before, was theirs! The five men swore each other to secrecy, intending to stake their claim when the mountain was accessible in the spring. But their brief encounter with the mountain treasure was too much of a temptation during the long winter to remain a secret. By the spring of 1867, three hundred men from Fort Union were poised to assault the mountain. Many of those, anticipating quick riches, were from southern states, Confederate veterans of the Civil War. A year and a half earlier, Union armies had forced their surrender. Their homelands were devastated and their economy in ruins. Westward migration provided a hope for the future.

Controlling the Chaos

By definition, a gold rush conjures to the imagination a wild, frenetic invasion of all types of humanity: prospectors racing to establish claims; merchants hastily building stores to supply their needs; tent cities dotting a once unspoiled land; claim jumpers hoping to make a quick strike before being detected; saloons, gambling rooms, dance halls and brothels ready to provide entertainment in return for a pinch of gold; and outlaws and con men looking for a fast dollar. Mix all these ingredients in various proportions, and this is what the Moreno Valley looked like in the spring of 1867. One miner declared that northern New Mexico would be "another California."

Those immediately affected by this surging tide of events were the native tribes living in the area and the owner of the land on which the gold was discovered, Lucien Bonaparte Maxwell. The Moache Utes and the Jicarilla Apaches resented the intrusion but could do little about it. Within ten years, the federal government would relocate the tribes far from the Valley.

Maxwell knew the invasion could not be stopped and proceeded to make the best of it. Unlike John Sutter, who gained little from the discovery of gold on his California property, Maxwell resolved to take advantage of the bonanza. He was owner of the vast Beaubien-Miranda Land Grant that extended from the Moreno Valley into southern Colorado. He established lease agreements with the miners, charging a dollar a month for placer claims and one-half of the year's profits from the lode claims. He also built his own mining operation on Baldy Mountain calling it the Aztec. Matthew Lynch and Tom Foley, while working the placer fields east of the mountain, received credit for discovering the lode.

By May 1867, four hundred claims owned by seventeen companies had been filed, all within an eight-mile radius of Baldy. By winter, this escalated to 1,280 claims. The miners realized that a governing body needed to be established if their claims were to be operated in an orderly and legal manner. Among the first gold rush participants were the officers and men from Ft. Union. Colonel Edward Bergmann established a claim called Spanish Bar. The Michigan Company, commanded by John Codlin, found gold on the flats of the Moreno Valley. The civilian miners looked to the military to provide the order needed to ensure peaceful prospecting. On May 13th, Codlin was elected chairman of an organizing committee whose duty was to establish rules regulating the filing of claims, water and timber rights, bills of sale and property deeds. William O'Neill was elected recorder for a two-year term. One proviso the miners insisted upon was that all documentation be available for public inspection.

A Town is Born

But what of Captain Moore, William Kroenig and their three companions? Their vowed secret was now known throughout the southwest. What did they reap from their discovery? Bronson, Kissinger, and Kelley returned to the Discovery Tree to find others already working their claim at Willow Creek. Bronson laid out five 200-foot claims from the Discovery Tree and called the operation Arthur and Company. Kissinger and Kelley worked the claims along with Bronson. On the other hand, Moore and Kroenig were businessmen of greater vision. They saw themselves as providers and investors rather than laborers in the mining operations. Moore put his sutler experience at Ft. Union to good use, establishing a mercantile business. Kroenig built a sawmill and became a partner with Lucien Maxwell. Lumber was in great demand for the construction of flumes, sluice boxes and housing. They produced 4,000 feet of finished lumber per day, easily selling all they could manufacture at inflated prices.

William Moore saw that the disorganized squatter community in the Moreno Valley could hardly be accepted as a town of importance and proceeded to call a meeting with other prominent business people, suggesting that the valley floor be surveyed and divided into lots. His proposal met with enthusiastic response, and surveyor T.G. Rowe was commissioned to plat the town. Paying tribute to Moore, the local citizens decided to name the town honoring his four-year old daughter, Elizabeth Catherine. So "Elizabethtown" was born, and the proud bearer of that name would live in the Valley until her death in 1934. Like other places of multi-syllable names, the locals developed a contraction for simpler speaking, and Elizabethtown became "E'Town."

The Town That Didn't Make It

In that summer of 1867, Lucien Maxwell observed remarkable changes in the newly formed Elizabethtown, which included a commercial district of five stores with twenty more under construction. Wide streets provided easy access to and from commercial and residential lots. Captain Moore had the bright idea, Maxwell thought, so why not build my own town? It seemed like an easy and profitable venture. His income from the placer leases alone was over $1,200 a month, a handsome sum in 1867 when the average worker made about $300 a year. Maxwell had money to invest. His gold extracted from Baldy that first spring and summer amounted to $100,000. Not equal to California, but considering all the start-up work and expenses, an impressive sum.

Maxwell had built the towns of Rayado and Cimarron, some 40 miles east along the northern route of the Santa Fe Trail, with great success. And now he had a new venture with gold, rather than wagon trains, as a source of income. But what shall I call my town? If Moore can name a town after his daughter, then I'll do the same! But I shall not call it a "town." It will be called a "city." So, Maxwell coined the name "Virginia City," honoring *his* favorite daughter.

Maxwell selected a site in the Moreno Valley located six miles east of E'Town, close to the entrance of Cimarron Canyon, with a survey of 400 lots. The location seemed ideal because the canyon road was the main trade route into the Valley. He announced a public auction scheduled for January 6, 1868. Any real estate person knows there are good and bad seasons for selling. At an elevation of 8,400 feet, dead winter in the Moreno Valley did not constitute a "good season." To compound matters, the winter signaled an exodus from the Valley because the miners were unable to work their claims.

Virginia City had no commercial district. The only structure was a tent … the sales office. By March, a handful of partially constructed, roofless houses were built but never completed. By the middle of summer, no one was willing to isolate themselves from the commerce and comforts of E'Town. The April 18th, 1868 edition of the *Santa Fe Weekly Gazette* quoted an E'Town resident who reflected the general attitude in a homespun metaphor: "Virginia City moved up here yesterday. Came up on a burro; says it's too lonesome down there and can't stand it; had to go three miles to speak to anyone."

Two years later, Maxwell's favorite daughter, Virginia, caused him great anguish when she secretly married an army officer, forsaking family and religion for love. The demise of Virginia City was perhaps an omen of this greater disappointment in Maxwell's life. In 1870, he decided to sell his nearly two-million acres and move elsewhere.

The Boom Years

On present day Highway 38, five miles northwest of Eagle Nest, County Road B-20 announces the entrance to Elizabethtown. Stop and scan the horizon to the south for the remnants of a stone structure which, in its heyday, was a prominent landmark—the Mutz Hotel, which was originally built by the Story Family. It is hard to believe that this ghostly landscape was once proposed to replace Santa Fe as the state capital! Note: In 2021 the only publicly accessible remains of Elizabethtown is the cemetery.

Let's return to the glory years when an ounce of gold panned from a gully was equal to a month's wage.

Two things were necessary for E'Town to be successful: improved transportation and an abundant water supply. Lucien Maxwell built a toll road through Cimarron Canyon connecting the Moreno Valley to southern Colorado. Another toll road through Raton Pass was constructed by "Uncle Dick" Wootton on land leased from Maxwell, reaching Trinidad, the destination for gold shipments from the Moreno Valley.

Santa Fe Trail wagons carried mining machinery and tools vital for the removal of gold from the placer and lode deposits. The wagons brought consumer products, encouraging more merchants to open stores, giving E'Town the appearance of a prosperous and permanent community. Some disdained the use of E'Town, preferring to call the locale "Elizabeth City." Names such as Gottlieb, Uhlfelder, and Froelick became synonymous with mercantile enterprises. Trail wagons provided an array of luxury items, such as champagne and oysters, to the saloons. The Montezuma Bar and Club Rooms, the Miner's Inn, and the Senate were popular drinking and gambling places.

V.S. Shelby of Santa Fe began a stage line through the Cimarron Canyon. By the spring of 1868, his Moreno Valley Stage and Freight Line provided daily service to Cimarron. The stage brought investors, mail service and, as one eager bachelor put it, "With a concord coach for conveyance, we will expect ladies." The fare was eight dollars. On the return trip, the stage carried gold destined for deposit in Trinidad. If children were making the trip, gold would be sewn into their clothing to avoid detection in the event of a holdup. So successful was Shelby that another line was inaugurated to Taos and Santa Fe.

The water problem was more complicated than the necessary upgrades in transportation. The natural flow for placer mining lasted only a few months. The placer fields extended 8-10 miles wide. The claims were so close to each other and so dense that recording maps had the look of a busy plaid. The gold was there but the lack of water, especially for hydraulic mining, caused the fields to lay dormant.

Army engineer, Captain Nichols S. Davis, was commissioned to find a solution. In the spring of 1868, he outlined an impressive plan: Tap the headwaters of the Red River (eleven miles to the west) and build a series of ditches, aqueducts, and sidehill flumes, bringing the precious water to the placer and lode operations in the Moreno Valley. When the survey was completed in May, it was calculated that the actual construction distance, given the topography, would be forty-one miles.

The "Big Ditch," as it began to be called, would have to contour around the north end of the Moreno Valley. Three miles of sidehill flumes had to be built. For five miles, bedrock ten feet deep had to be removed to create a ditch. The longest aqueduct had a span of 2,376 feet across a canyon near Red River Pass at an elevation of 79 feet above a creek bed. Imagine eight football fields set in a line, located eight stories above ground level! Captain Davis' West Point training in the field of engineering had a formidable challenge. Davis estimated that 7.65 million gallons of water per day would flow through the Big Ditch. Undaunted by the immensity of the project, local citizens invested $250,000 to assure its construction. Lucien Maxwell was the major contributor.

The incredible fact was that the Big Ditch was completed in six months! Nothing in New Mexico had seen its like. Winter was now setting in, so the eagerly awaited flow was delayed until July of the following year. Martin and Scott's Humbug Gulch, considered to be the richest placer deposit, first received the water. Imagine their disappointment when the flow produced only 15% of Davis' original calculation. The Big Ditch was plagued by leakage and evaporation problems. The investors then began to play "hot potato." The majority sold their unprofitable shares to Colonel V.S. Shelby whose stagecoach lines were a financial success. But Shelby couldn't solve the Big Ditch's problems and sold his shares to Maxwell.

Shortly before his death in 1875, Maxwell sold the Ditch to a brilliant young geologist and civil engineer, Matthew Lynch. Lynch had discovered the highly profitable Aztec Lode and was one of the more successful miners in the valley. He modernized the design and repaired the problem areas, turning the Ditch into a successful venture. Tragically, five years later, he was killed by a falling tree. His brothers tried to continue the operation; however, by 1880, hydraulic mining declined. Twelve years of intensive work had depleted the placer fields. Such colorful names as Grouse, Humbug, Muddy, Red Bandanna, Golden Ajax, Mystic, French Henry, and Legal Tender were claims now quiet. The days of easy pickings were gone. Some vestiges of the Big Ditch remain today … a mute legacy to an extraordinary engineering adventure.

A Comet in The Sky

Just as the heavens provide a fleeting glimpse of extraordinary activity, so did the life of Elizabethtown reach awesome proportions only to fade after a brief time of luster. By 1868, the second year of gold prospecting, one hundred buildings were constructed. By the end of the summer, 3,000 men were working the gold fields. Estimates of its peak population range from 6,000 to 10,000. Historians generally consider 7,000 to be a more reliable figure.

Lots were selling for $800-$1,200 per lot. Multiply that by at least 20 times to appreciate the value in today's dollar. Ethnic segregation was a way of life. Spanish Mexicans had their own community called Chihuahua Town or Mexican Town. It is estimated that as many as 1,000 lived in this enclave. Another important "suburb" of E'Town was Baldy Town located on Mt. Baldy itself where Maxwell's Aztec and Montezuma Mines were located. Rich placer fields north of the Moreno Valley along the eastern slopes of the mountain made it more convenient for the prospectors to live there. Its peak population in 1871 was about 500.

The citizens of E'Town recognized the financial power now focused on the Moreno Valley, but they craved more than wealth. Political prestige and social class became paramount goals. Without a doubt, the fledgling community could claim to be the most important city north of Santa Fe. Political recognition soon followed.

In January 1869, eighteen months after E'Town came into existence, the state legislature created a new county named in honor of United States Vice President elect, Schuyler Colfax. Colfax was a well-known and popular politician whose backers predicted that one day he would be President. The scandals of the Grant administration ruined his career.

The new county not only included E'Town and the Maxwell Land Grant, but extended east to the Texas border, including what are now Harding and Union Counties. The logical site for the county seat was Elizabethtown. Local voters overwhelmingly approved the idea. A year later, E'Town became the first incorporated city in New Mexico.

Its political base firmly established, E'Town now proceeded to develop its social graces. The Moreno Hotel opened with an inaugural featuring the finest foods and champagne. Henry Lambert, whose presence would grace the county for over 50 years, built the E'Town Hotel. Its popularity made Lambert a fortune. In the summer of 1869, the first newspaper, *The Moreno Lantern*, was published, followed by two other papers, *The Elizabethtown Telegraph* and *The Elizabethtown Argus*. During their short-lived existence, the newspapers reported in great detail about local social occasions, from weddings to civic celebrations. Their exuberant and flowery language promoted the graces of Elizabethtown society.

In 1868 further evidence of maturity came to E'Town. The Methodist-Episcopal Conference of Colorado sent a missionary, the Rev. J.L. Dyer, to preach in the Elizabethtown area. According to the Conference records, he found that civility was more veneer than substance. E'Town was basically a wild, brawling mining town. He preached to small audiences, sometimes to only a single family. He made six converts, but they all moved away. He constructed a little board shanty, with the bedroom, parlor, kitchen, and study in one room. The other room was reserved for his horse, an essential tool for the gospel in those days. Conference records indicate that during the years of his Elizabethtown ministry, Rev. Dyer traveled 10,000 miles on horseback. By 1870, a small church building 24x26x18 feet was constructed on two lots, thanks to a donor. Rev. Dyer recorded that: "Attendance was meager … and some of the members worthless. It was a rough time. Shooting and killing were very common."

Elizabethtown poet and rancher James Gallagher composed his impression of the ministry in E'Town:

"Still farther on was the little church,
Several benches out on the porch,
Windows were closed, doors seldom touched,
It seemed this place wasn't patronized much."

Crime And Punishment

If the Methodist-Episcopal Conference of Colorado had visited the Rev. Dyer's ministry, they would have noted his comment "shootings and killings are very common" to be accurate. In 1868 the town's seven saloons and three dance halls outnumbered the five mercantile stores. Saloon bars were often 100-200 feet in length with ladies of easy virtue ready to greet the customers. The grubby-looking, exhausted miners with their pouches of gold were the magnet that drew all strata of humanity to this new El Dorado. In one 24-hour period, there were eight killings, all isolated confrontations caused by a variety of motives.

The first elected sheriff of E'Town was H.J. Calhoun. His career was not a distinguished one. He had plenty to keep him busy but was ineffectual in bringing order to the community. So prevalent were outlaws and troublemakers that wives placed loaded shotguns inside their doors while their men were working the placer fields.

Matters became so bad in that first year of E'Town's existence that the inevitable happened—Vigilante Justice. Frustrated by the general condition of lawlessness, a group of citizens formed a committee to solve the problem. The name of every known outlaw or troublemaker was written on a poker chip and placed in a cigar box. Committee members entered a darkened room, taking a chip from the box. After reading the name inscribed, they returned the chips to the box without comment. Then another cigar box was presented containing black chips equal to the number of men in the room. One of the chips in this box had a white dot. The one selecting the white dotted chip had the duty of eliminating the man he selected in the previous drawing. Everyone in town knew of this ritual. Sometimes the name of the troublemaker selected would be leaked. It was not uncommon to see a man, for no apparent reason, quickly saddle his horse and leave town.

Not all members of the vigilante group were altruistic. Saloon keeper Joseph Herberger used his power for personal vengeance. To settle a personal quarrel, Herberger made accusations against a certain Pony O'Neil saying he was guilty of murder elsewhere in the state. Innocent of all charges, O'Neil nevertheless became a candidate for the poker chip drawing. Herberger delighted in carrying out the task, bashing O'Neil's head with a brick and then calling his fellow vigilantes to hang the alleged culprit. The still conscious O'Neil protested his innocence, but his cries were silenced with a hail of bullets as he dangled from a rope.

When the truth of the incident became known, the vigilantes were ashamed but justified their action saying it was a lesson to the community that they meant business. Herberger was not brought to justice and continued his hatred and bullying ways. He was finally arrested and convicted of a personal vendetta killing of another saloon keeper, but he spent only two years in the Territorial Penitentiary in Santa Fe.

Another sad commentary of vigilante justice occurred when a local Mexican was arrested by the sheriff on a murder charge. To ensure a fair trial, the sheriff arranged for a change of venue to the town of Mora. The angry vigilantes stormed the jail, captured the accused man, and hung him from a tree. They tacked a card to the body which read: "So much for the change of venue."

Stagecoach robberies were a constant concern. The gold they carried to Trinidad was the life blood of the town. One way to control the problem was to offer substantial rewards for the capture of the highwaymen—dead or alive. "Long Tom" Taylor was a 6'7" E'Town thug. Jailed for murder, he managed to escape and joined partnership with "Coal-Oil Jimmy." They decided to go big time by robbing gold shipments. Their favorite place of attack was a narrow gap in the Cimarron Canyon called the Palisades. So successful were their holdups that a $3,000 reward was offered for their capture. The handsome sum attracted the interest of Joe McCurdy and John Stewart, who became members of the gang in order to wait for the opportunity to collect the reward money. One day they drove into E'Town in an old farm wagon containing the heaped bodies of Long Tom and Coal-Oil Jimmy. Their first stop was at the office of the local attorney to make sure they had the right to collect the reward.

The most bizarre chain of criminal events occurred in 1870. E'Town was familiar with a huge, full-bearded man who came to town for supplies. His Ute wife and child stayed in the wagon motionless, speaking to no one. The man conducted his business and then drove to his cabin along Nine Mile Creek at the base of Palo Flechado Pass. The townspeople viewed the occasional visits of the three solitary figures with little interest. The man's name was Charles Kennedy.

One night in September, Pearson's Saloon was filled with cowboys and miners drinking their way through a severe rainstorm. Holding court was a rancher, Clay Allison. His fame as a gunman, hard drinker, and vigilante justice activist extended as far away as Dodge City. When he rode into town, the newspaper recorded the event. He usually made news. Now the news came to him. The saloon door flew open and there stood Kennedy's wife, barefoot, bloody, and soaked with rain. It was evident that she had been beaten, fearfully running the nine miles to E'Town to seek safety.

She told a horrible story. In a fit of temper, her husband had killed her 10-year-old son by swinging his body against the stone fireplace.

Allison grabbed her and took her to the stove where she could receive some warmth. For all of his rough ways, he had a reputation of being kind and gentle with women. His southern background fumed with disgust at what Kennedy had done. Feeling a sense of security, the wife told the whole series of events which led to her flight. No one had heard such a grisly story before.

Kennedy would invite travelers to stay in their cabin before embarking on the 20-mile journey to Taos. It seemed like a hospitable invitation before attempting the arduous journey through the canyon. After giving the stranger his fill of liquor, Kennedy would kill the victim, rob him of his valuables and throw the body into the cellar until he could later dispose of it by cremation. The wife said the property was full of bones; that Kennedy had done this many times and forced her to help him dispose of the remains. Kennedy only killed strangers traveling to other destinations thereby avoiding any suspicion that he knew of their whereabouts. Her boy was killed earlier that day because he told a "guest" that bodies were under the floor. Kennedy killed the visitor before killing her boy. He then began to drink heavily until he passed out. That was how she was able to escape.

Allison formed a posse which rode full speed to Kennedy's cabin. They found Kennedy still drunk and hustled him to E'Town. Justice McBride began an investigation. A collection of bones, appearing to be human, was carried from the property for forensic examination by E'Town officials. The results were inconclusive. But as more evidence was discovered, including a complete skeleton with a gunshot hole in the head, it appeared that the wife's story was true.

Twenty-five vigilantes, under the leadership of Allison, decided to hold their own trial, convinced that Kennedy was guilty. They overpowered Kennedy's guards and proceeded to conduct their own version of justice.

Kennedy was allowed to select 12 men of the vigilante group as jurors. A young attorney, recently arrived from Michigan, volunteered to defend Kennedy. His name was Melvin W. Mills. This event would be only the first of Mills many roles in Territorial New Mexico history. Despite the guilty-prone assembly, Mills presented such a persuasive defense that the "jury" could not come to a decision. The frustrated vigilantes returned Kenney to his jail cell.

It now appeared that proper justice would take its course. But Allison would not be outdone. He rallied the mob, convincing them that Kennedy should be hung. On the night of October 7th, disguising their faces, they again overpowered Kennedy's guards, declared him guilty, and hung him from the rafter of the slaughterhouse. The coroner's jury declared that "death was by hanging, by parties unknown." The *Elizabethtown Press and Telegraph* editorialized in this fashion:

So ended the life of this cold-blooded assassin ... there is a general feeling of satisfaction that he is at last beyond the power of doing further harm ... still, while we have no pity for the murderer, we cannot commend the action of those who hung him. The time has passed when it was necessary for the people of this community to take the punishment of offenders into their own hands.

There is an epilogue to this story which appears to be more legend than fact. After the inquest, it is said that Allison and his sidekick, Davey Crockett, cut off Kennedy's head and impaled it on the picket fence in front of Henry Lambert's saloon as a warning to future malefactors. The head was stolen, eventually obtained by the Smithsonian Institute in Washington D.C. for study. There was a scientific theory at the time that the shape of the skull could determine or predict criminal behavior. Calls to the Institute could not confirm that Kennedy's head had ever been received or catalogued for study.

Elizabethtown In Transition

In 1870, E'Town was at the height of its success. The placer fields were rich in ore. Santa Fe Trail wagons brought an abundance of industrial and luxury goods. Despite the failure of the Big Ditch, E'Town drew thousands of Colorado miners whose gold fields were rapidly depleting. The town had its own mayor, city council, resident county recorder and judicial system. Despite breakdowns in law enforcement, the vigilantes, for all their faults, were there to maintain their version of order.

Then the unexpected happened. Lucien Maxwell decided to sell his vast Land Grant holdings, which included the Moreno Valley. He offered no explanation other than to say that he would buy the abandoned Ft. Sumner and adjacent Bosque Redondo land in the east-central part of the state. Maxwell's relationship with the thousands of migrants to the Valley had been an agreeable one. His lease arrangements with the miners were reasonable. His own mining operations had brought him immense wealth. Prior to the discovery of gold, his annual income was $10,000 a year. This was a large sum in the 1860s, but now his income was twenty times that amount.

He was not confrontational with those who refused to enter lease or sale agreements. Many of the migrants thought they had a natural right to work the land; "miner's rights" they called it. Ranchers like Clay Allison annexed land simply because it was there for the taking. The whole idea of a Mexican land grant of one and three-quarter million acres being the private property of one man was foreign to their thinking. After all, this was the edge of the western frontier where every man should find his destiny without interference.

Perhaps Maxwell looked back at his benign empire prior to the discovery of gold. Perhaps he decided to take his profits and control another land not affected by the convulsions which confronted him. A year later, a European consortium of British and Dutch investors bought the Grant, being assured that legal title as private property was firmly established. But their legal title would be called into question by no less than the federal government.

The new owners respected all prior Maxwell land agreements, provided some proof could be established. But they went after the squatters who refused to conform. The squatters claimed this was public land. The battle lines of the Colfax County War had been drawn. The new owners chose Cimarron as their headquarters, electing a local Board of Directors who were responsible for bringing the squatters into line. A spirit of antagonism and lawlessness pervaded E'Town. Mobs threatened to burn the city. The territorial governor sent troops to quell a riot. Military force calmed the day but not the anger of the insurgents. The riot played into the hands of the foreign consortium. E'Town's stability as the political center of the county was called into question. Two years later, the county seat was moved to Cimarron, which also happened to be the headquarters of the Maxwell Land Grant company.

Decline

Sometimes the decision of one man can serve as a metaphor for his surroundings. For three years, hotelier and saloon keeper Henry Lambert had made a fortune with his E'Town Hotel. He was a colorful Frenchman who claimed he had cooked and served meals to Abraham Lincoln and General U.S. Grant. He had a diplomatic way which more often than not diffused trouble. Gunfights would erupt in his establishment, but he was able to confine them to the antagonists, thus preserving the physical integrity of his saloon. When he saw trouble brewing, he would yell, "Drinks are on the house," creating such jubilation that real or apparent grievances were often forgotten. An astute businessman with an eye to the future, Lambert saw Cimarron as the town of destiny.

He closed his E'Town business in 1871 and moved close to the headquarters of the Maxwell Land Grant company, to Cimarron, which a year later would become the county seat. His St. James Hotel became famous throughout the West. Eventually, the St. James fell into disrepair after the railroad came through and effectively killed the Santa Fe trail, and as the gold in the area dwindled. After Lambert's death in 1913, the St. James continued to thrive for a number of years under the ownership of others before being closed for a while. From 1926–1985, the hotel passed from owner to owner, but in 1985 it was restored to its former glory. In January 2009 the hotel was purchased by the Express UU Bar Ranch, and it underwent another major renovation.

Meanwhile, E'Town suffered a major casualty as a result of the Colfax County War. (*See also Chapter 1, The Moreno Valley and the Colfax County War.*) It was the murder of Rev. Franklin J. Tolby. Tolby succeeded Rev. Dyer and became active in supporting squatters' rights on the land grant. Although

Tolby's residence was in Cimarron, he made regular Sunday trips to preach in E'Town. The moral force of his anti-grant position emboldened the squatters and embarrassed the grant owners.

In September 1875, Tolby was shot to death in the Cimarron Canyon while returning from Sunday services in E'Town. His horse and personal belongings were intact. The two wounds in his back had all the marks of assassination. Whoever was responsible for masterminding this killing misjudged the results. The squatters now revered Tolby as a martyr in a just cause. The public reputation of the land grant company disintegrated amid accusations that it was responsible for Tolby's murder. New leaders emerged to take Tolby's place, and the war dragged on for another twelve years. But E'Town would be spared the main cycle of violence as the eye of the storm moved to Cimarron and the newly created railroad towns of Raton and Springer.

So, the comet's glow began to dim. Without large amounts of water, the gold in the placer fields couldn't be extracted. Lode mining became very expensive because the ore produced was lower quality. Threats by the land grant "regulators" caused some squatters to pack up and move on. By 1875 the bonanza days were only a memory, but many of the old timers stayed on.

A 1901 E'Town photograph records the presence of six pioneers who arrived in 1867: Joseph Lowery, Herman Froelick, John Pearson, J.W. Williams, A.J. Raught, and Thomas Richey. Elizabeth Moore became the town's schoolteacher. It was a quiet time compared to the days of her childhood. Baldy, sometimes called Elizabeth Peak, was silent now. Some mining continued, but the Moreno Valley residents concentrated on more enduring ventures: ranching and farming.

The Comet Returns

In 1887 the United States Supreme Court finally resolved the Colfax County War crisis, by declaring the Maxwell Grant to be valid private property. The owners could now promote a massive advertising campaign seeking land buyers without fearing legal opposition. Conditions had changed substantially since the beginning of the war.

The railroad was now a reality. The Santa Fe Railroad created a north-south spine of tracks from Raton to Deming. Spur lines provided east-west access. There was talk about a line being built from Springer to Cimarron, extending to Ute Park. Maybe the line would continue through Cimarron Canyon and reach the Moreno Valley. Wagon transportation was reduced to local, not transcontinental business.

Now known as the Maxwell Land Grant and Railway Company, its board of directors offered land and mining rights at bargain prices. Corporations, utilizing the railroad's ability to haul heavy equipment cheaply, reopened mining operations in the Baldy district. E'Town soon boasted a population of 1,200.

These were gentler days than the brawling 1860s. A few outlaws such as train robber Tom "Black Jack" Ketchum and his Hole-In-The-Wall Gang frequented the town, particularly Moore's Saloon, causing some disturbances but nothing like during the old days.

Ketchum lived two lives. He had a ranch at La Belle, not far from E'Town and, while he could be mean and obstreperous, gave no clue of his other life. It did seem strange, however, that he would flash hundred-dollar bills while enjoying all-night poker games at the saloon. The town couldn't account for his periodic disappearances for weeks at a time. This was when he was out robbing trains. After one robbery, he carried a wounded companion, Black Bob McManus, to a ranch six miles south of E'Town, sending for a doctor and provisions. When a posse came into town looking for the gang, the truth became known, but everyone kept silent for fear of reprisal. Ketchum was captured and hanged in Clayton in 1901. After his execution, the townspeople delighted in telling stories about Black Jack and his E'Town connection.

As E'Town began to attract more settlers, transportation services were reestablished. The Springer and Moreno Valley Stage Line began daily runs in 1894. A competing line, the Moreno Valley Stage and Freight Company, also prospered, carrying 220 passengers per month at $5 per person. A newspaper, *The Northern New Mexico Miner*, appeared in 1896 with uninterrupted publishing until 1902. There were no lynchings and few shootings. Church, school, and social events dominated the news. The three hotels were doing good business: Nadock's Moreno Hotel, Herman Mutz's Story Hotel and the Miner's Inn. The school established a drama

LURE, LORE AND LEGENDS

society. The town was equally proud of its Cornet Band with instruments manufactured in New York City.

Miners looked at the introduction of industrial-sized hydraulic systems to control and recycle water consumption. Two new ideas emerged. One was dredging the valley floor along the Moreno River. The other was to dig a tunnel horizontally from one end of Baldy Mountain to the other, hoping to strike the mountain's mother lode.

The dredging idea was proposed by Henry A. Argue and an investment group from Buffalo, New York. They assembled a dredging machine constructed on a steam powered railroad car. A minimal amount of water was used. The project did not produce sufficient profit and was abandoned. But the idea had merit, thought H.J. Reiling of Chicago. What was needed was a different approach. Perhaps he was reminded that the Big Ditch began as a failure but became successful under the leadership of Matthew Lynch. Reiling's idea was to utilize as much water as possible by damming the Moreno River and creating a lake.

He formed the Oro Dredging Company in 1900, designing a massive contraption with huge boilers and hundreds of wheels. Built in the Midwest, the monster machine was dismantled, shipped by railroad to Springer and by wagon through the Cimarron Canyon to the Moreno River. By August 1901, everything was in place. The local population looked with awe at this giant machine with its claws ready to attack the riverbed.

Reiling had a lady friend visiting from the east coast whom he described as "a precious stone, a diamond in her home." Her name was Eleanor Robinson. He named the dredge "The Eleanor" in her honor. H.J. was not above a bit of theatrics for its public relations value. He decided that a christening ceremony would be in order. To perform the honor, he chose Mrs. W.A. Maughey who he called "the loveliest pearl that fair Ohio had produced." Mrs. Maughey did not disappoint him. Her christening prayer was worthy of the finest ship steaming the ocean: "With the authority given me by the powers that be, I christen thee, Eleanor. May thy wheels never turn without profit to thy owners; may there be no loss of gold to thy owners; may there be no leakage in thy seams, May harmony and success prevail."

The celebration and showmanship was a large success. Now it was

The remains of the Mutz Hotel highlights the E'Town landscape. Completed in 1905, it replaced the Story Hotel destroyed in the 1903 fire. (photo by Elaine Jarzen)

the duty of Eleanor's 21,000-pound boilers to produce enough power for her buckets to dig 15 feet into the riverbed and deposit her catch in long sluice boxes which reached to the shore. To everyone's delight, Eleanor was a success. She was producing $1,000 a day in gold. At one time in her career, she was producing one-third of all the gold mined in New Mexico.

But Eleanor's success was her downfall. Her owners became greedy and decided to commission another dredge in Colorado, confident that Eleanor's success could be repeated elsewhere. Eleanor was mortgaged to finance the Colorado dredge. Her new sister was a dismal failure. The company was bankrupt.

In the four years of service Eleanor had dredged $200,000 worth of gold. Sold in 1906, she never operated again. She was purchased by Charles Springer on behalf of the Land Grant Company. The lake created by Reiling was drained, and Eleanor sunk into the soil and disappeared from view in the 1940s.

Tenacity and perseverance could be the nicknames of the McIntyre brothers, Alexander and William. For 36 years, they bored a tunnel into Baldy Mountain, hoping to reach the mother lode. Because placer deposits were found on every side of the mountain, they theorized that a tunnel would reach the source of the gold. "Billy" and Al formed the Deep Tunnel and Mining Company in 1900, drilling their tunnel 2,000 feet below the summit. Another tunnel was started on the opposite side of the mountain, the purpose being that the two would join. They were good engineers because when the two tunnels did join, they were only six inches apart. Billie died six years before the tunnel was completed, but it made no difference. The mother lode was never discovered, if indeed, there had been one at all.

The Demise
In 1903 a disastrous fire engulfed E'Town, destroying many of the buildings. The fire broke out in Remsberg's log store, probably from a defective flue. The flames spread to the Mutz Hotel, Harry Brainard's saloon, Remsberg's warehouse, and Gottlieb and Uhlfelder's general store. The Moreno Hotel was ignited from flying embers and within an hour, all these buildings lay in ashes. Only Herman Froelick's mercantile store survived.

Despite Eleanor's success and high hopes for the McIntyre venture, the town never seemed to recover. Herman Mutz remained optimistic, rebuilding his hotel in stone. At the same time, weather patterns were changing for the worse. A series of severe winter snowstorms brought the town to a halt, creating almost famine conditions. Ranchers lost 50% of their livestock. It seemed that nature was conspiring with manmade disasters to squeeze life from the town's efforts to revitalize itself.

Other substantial changes provided options which did not exist before. Charles and Frank Springer proposed the building of a dam near the entrance to Cimarron Canyon. A partially completed railroad tunnel into the Valley would have to be abandoned if the Springer project was approved. It was approved, and Eagle Nest Lake came into existence.

Talmage Neal bought property next to the lake and founded the town of Therma. Although the lake was originally designed as a water irrigation project, it had more success as a fishing and tourist attraction. E'Town people began dismantling their wooden structures and moving to the new town. In 1908, placer mining on Baldy was suspended because of water pollution problems. Furthermore, the Maxwell Land Company tightened its mining policies. One had to buy the land before claiming mining rights. Small investors or individual prospectors were squeezed out of participation. The second resurgence of E'Town was now disappearing.

Ironically, by that time Baldy Town near the top of the mountain had a greater population than E'Town. The land grant company continued

The E'Town Museum when it was operating.
(photo by Elaine Jarzen)

to have faith in the Aztec Mine, located next to Baldy Town. Operations continued with limited success until the 1940s. In 1962 the acreage along the eastern slope of Baldy was purchased and donated to the Philmont Boy Scout Ranch. The vestiges of what once were major mining operations, as well as the remnants of Baldy Town, are entrusted to the Philmont Ranch for historical preservation.

Elizabethtown in Modern Times

When German immigrant Herman Mutz arrived in the Moreno Valley in 1881, he would have no idea that his family would preserve what remains of E'Town into the 21st century. In 1886, Herman married Tena Story, the adopted daughter of Chancey and Augusta Story. The Storys owned the hotel, and the newlyweds took over management. They also started a cattle ranch. The couple had ten children, two of which, Adolph and Emil, joined in their father's ranching business. When Herman died, a third brother (George) joined in the business. Some of the descendants of the Herman Mutz family have remained in E'Town and the Mutz property has been divided among some of the Herman Mutz descendants over the years.

In an attempt to preserve E'Town's heritage, Beni-Jo Fulton, the step-daughter of Robert Mutz, operated a museum for several years in one of the original buildings. As mentioned elsewhere, in 2021 the E'Town Cemetery is the only portion of the original town that is accessible to the public. The cemetery is located on a high knoll with a spectacular view of the Valley floor and Baldy Mountain. If you visit, let the ghosts speak to you and imagine in your mind's eye what this bustling, brawling El Dorado must have been like.

Editor's Note: When local newspapers publicized the Moreno Valley Writers Guild history project, Joanne Teagarden of Taos Canyon called, saying she had found some material which might be of interest in an attic trunk owned by her deceased aunt. Among the items was this poem composed by James H. Gallagher (1898-1967). Gallagher grew up in Elizabethtown as a youth. He was the brother-in-law of Mae Lowrey Gallagher, whose mother was Elizabeth Moore Lowrey, after whom E'Town was named. I contacted the Gallagher family who told me they were not aware of the poem's existence. This enjoyable bit of verse in irregular iambics and couplets names and describes the residents and their activities in the most familiar and sometimes critical terms. It is printed here with the permission of the Gallagher family. —Jack C. Urban.

Old "E" Town, New Mexico
by
James H. Gallagher
Eagle Nest, New Mexico

I'd love to take a trip to my old home town,
Although they say it is badly run down.
The houses and fences have all been wrecked
The streets with cans are all bespect.

On old Moreno, way up in the hills,
Mountains rocks, and beautiful rills;
A place that was known to the Indian alone,
Until the paleface came to make his home.

In the days of old the miners bold,
Found this place, and discovered gold.
Gamblers came, it was a place of fame,
With card tables many, and the poker game.

In the days to follow, it was a busy place,
It was a lucky man who won the race;
For many a man was left in the brush,
During the days of that gold rush.

A little old town in a wonderful land
Way back in the mountains, Oh so grand!
Old Baldy Peak above timber line high,
In the pines below, the cool breezes sigh.

The little town grew by bounds and leaps,
But now it's quiet, the old place sleeps.
The Old Timers are gone and most forgotten,
What houses that's left, are most all rotten.

The Town was named after Elizabeth Moore,
First white child born on Moreno shore.
Who to Joseph Lowrey was united one morn;
To this happy union seven children were born.

A Tenderfoot from Kentucky, a Doctor Bass,
Won the heart of the oldest lass.
Doc had an office on the side of the hill.
And if you got sick, he'd give you a pill.

Then Chas Gallagher, a pretty good Pal,
Took the heart and hand of the second Gal.
Charlie didn't work in any darn mine,
But he's all right, and doing fine.

Along came John Haddow, to try a whirl,
And the rascal took another girl.
John had a truck and carried the mail;
To get thru, he'd seldom if ever fail.

Then came T.D. Neal, they call him Tal,
He won the heart of the youngest Gal.
T.D. runs a store at the forks of the road,
And for candies and groceries, he can give you a load.

Joe Lowrey, Jr. is the oldest lad,
In many ways resembles his Dad.
He used to think he was bully of town,
But he got married and settled down.

William Lowrey, the youngest lad,
Is following the footsteps of his Dad.
He is always digging, hunting gold,
Just as the miners did of old.

In this Old Town there were several stores,
A saloon at no less than a dozen doors;
Also the Mutz Hotel and Miners Inn,
And the Red Front Stable, they kept horses in.

H.H. Hankins ran the stage coach line.
And often got in with the mail on time.
Swearinger and Hubanks made the trip,
They generally got in, if they did not slip.

There was the freighter, Old George Spinner,
A happy go lucky, whistling sinner.
Freighted summer, winter, all kinds of weather.
With the darndest crow baits that ever stretched leather.

Johnie McIntosh ran the Miners Inn,
The way he put up grub was sure a sin.
He'd feed the bums all they could eat,
Then throw the devils out on the street.

Just over the street was Froelick's Store.
Chip Chapman lived on the second floor.
Chappy was teacher of our school,
But he never showed up on April Fool.

Remsburg's place was a corner store
With an old dance hall on the upper floor.
Pete Perry worked in Remsburg's place,
A nice old fellow with a whiskered face.

Cahills Drug Store handled the drugs
That people needed to kill the bugs.
L.L. Cahill was the Town doctor too,
But the doctor cases were darn few.

The Montezuma Bar, just over the way,
There Frank Derrick had his wheel in play.
When the boys dropped in the wheel to play,
Frank would take their roll away.

While out in front at the old hitch racks,
With cowboy saddles upon their backs,
The horses stood in the burning sun,
While the boys inside were having fun.

Pearson's store on the side of the hill,
A saloon underneath that was never still.
This was the place the miners hung around
If they weren't out shooting up the Town.

Julius Whlelder clerked at Gotleib's place
When he wasn't out on another case.
If the day was cold or very hot,
He generally slipped out to get a shot.

Bennet and Weber ran the butcher shop,
A log foundation with a frame on top.
They sawed all day, made no stops,
Served anything there from horn to chops.

Herman Funk had a barber shop where
He jerked out your whiskers, pulled your hair.
The people thought he was off in the bean;
He was trying to build a flying machine!

Up on the hill was the old Garrick Hall.
Every Saturday night, there was a grand ball.
At the start of the music, you'd go into a trance.
Dutch Henry and Gallagher played for the dance.

Farther up the hill was the Moreno Hotel,
Run by Herberger, who sold liquor as well.
This old mansion was built of logs.
In the backyard, was burros and dogs.

Still farther on was the little church.
Several benches out on the porch;
Windows were closed, doors seldom touched.
It seemed this place wasn't patronized much.

Around the rocks in Mexican Town
Pearson and Hayward had a saloon;
The last chance out and the first chance in,
To get a drink of wine, whiskey, or gin.

Herman Mutz ran the Mutz Hotel.
At times the boarders didn't fare so well.
They had to climb stairs to get to bed,
And oft time failed to make it, so they said.

Mutz also had a livery barn;
Had some hogs from off the farm.
We often rode those hogs at night
If we couldn't watch a drunken fight.

Judge Carrington was the Town J.P.,
And big Charlie Drake the Deputy.
We wasn't allowed out on the street
Unless we could outrun big Charlie's feet.

One night Charlie throwed me in jail,
He told on me an untrue tale.
We went to Websters to do a tick tack,
I ran around to hide in the back.

It was close to the two by four jail.
On one side of this was a hog pen stale;
Built of cans and rotten logs,
This was where McIntosh kept his hogs.

It was for this place I made a dive,
When out came Johnie with his 45.
There I was with them darn hogs,
All tangled up in cans and rotten logs.

I tried to explain it was all in fun,
He said that's all right, don't try to run.
Then Drake threw me in jail
Said I was trying to steal hogs from a pen so stale.

One evening after the sun had gone down,
The Mutz Hotel we had gathered round.
From the walk in front, we had taken planks,
We meant no harm, just playing pranks.

It made Herman sore, so he got his gun,
Started throwing lead at us on the run.
He knew how to handle that old gat,
At the very first shot I lost a good hat.

But I'll never knock on that old Town,
It was a darn nice place to hang around,
And many a night had a lot of fun
We tin canned burros to see them run.

There were a few around like there always is,
Who never tell anyone about their biz.
I guess Long John was one of these.
He didn't work much, but done as he pleased.

Charlie Carter was another guy.
He didn't worry if chops were high;
Always had plenty to spend,
And often some poor devil a five he'd lend.

There was John McGovern and Pat O'Malley
Who pulled off a fight out in the alley.
I don't know who came out on top
When I saw that fight I couldn't stop.

Orie DeLong, a rounder, worked on the dredge.
He was the pilot and held the edge
Over the rest of the boys on that old boat
That tore up the river while she was afloat.

On the dredge Geo Downey was a handyman,
Carried a hammer and some nails in a can.
George was a carpenter, a pretty good scout,
And worked a little when the boss wasn't out.

Poor McGovern on the old wood scow,
They sure worked him plenty, and how.
He'd load up with wood, start for the boat,
The wood line would break, leaving him afloat.

Kamerer was last to own the Montezuma Saloon,
And ran it for years after the boom.
Jake had all kinds of liquor upon the shelf,
But drank darn little, if any, himself.

Tom Clouser sat round in a chair all day.
Tommie was a good shoemaker, in a way.
Sometimes for Jake, he would tend bar,
His private bottle was old three star.

Sam Boyd, Englishman, worked at the tunnel.
When he called for a drink, they gave him a funnel.
He'd come downtown to have a big time,
But seldom, if ever, would he spend a dime.

There was Otto Mueller, another guy,
I never could figure how he got by.
He did work a little in the mine,
But hung around Jake's most of the time.

Joe Cannard, miner and bear hunter, too,
He killed some bear, but darn few.
Dug little holes wherever he went.
Always broke, never had a cent.

Old Jack Murphy was another character,
Always tight if he had the liquor.
He'd set them up for the whole darn bunch,
Then he would buy a great big lunch.

This is the history from old "E" Town,
If you don't believe it, just inquire around
And you'll know what I say is mighty true;
I know what I'm talking about, I'll tell you.

When things slowed up in that old Town,
I drifted down to Old Cimarron;
Spent many years in that old place,
And they said round there, I was quite a case.

But all the time I've drifted round,
I have always longed for that old Town.
It wouldn't be the same, I know
As in the years so long ago.

But if the cards stay in the pack,
Again someday I'll be drifting back.
So I make this vow right here and now,
I am going back why — when — and how.

Brief Glimpses At the Valley

County Road B-9 and Lakeview Pines

by Mary Munch

(Editor's Note: Intersecting Highway 64 from Palo Flechado Pass to Eagle Nest, there are county roads of historical significance. Mary B. Munch, living in Grand Island, Nebraska, recalled from personal experience four generations of her family on County Road B-9, also known as Lakeview Pines.)

My parents and I first visited the valley in 1930 and stayed in cabins owned by the Matkin family which were located on the north side of County Road B-9 just at the tree line. They also owned the Laguna Vista Lodge which was located on the southwest corner of the intersection of County Road B-9 and Highway 64. It was a "U" shaped lodge with a large reception-living room area across the front facing the highway and bedroom wings stretching to the west. At one time, engineering students from Oklahoma A&M College (now Oklahoma State University) stayed in the lodge when they came for some of their off-campus summer classes. Some of the Necas girls worked there. Joe Necas lives in the family home part of the summer. The family home is ½ mile south of B-9, above B-7, just below the tree line.

The next owner of the Matkin cabins that I remember were people by the name of Leright. (I'm not sure of the spelling) and they had a caretaker, Mr. McFadden. They added a large barn and had riding horses and pack horses. It was possible at that time to obtain written permission from the Pueblo Indian Chief to take day trips and overnight trips to Pueblo Stream and Blue Lake to fish. Tourists came to the valley to make trips to this favorite fishing spot and the horses were in demand for these trips. I did not qualify as a licensed guide because I was not old enough nor was I a New Mexico citizen, but as an amateur guide I took several trips to this area. Another girl who was a licensed guide, Betty (I think her last name was Singer, or something similar) lived down on the highway.

After World War II, Leon George Gates and his wife Vivian bought the cabins that Matkin built, and Vivian named the area Lakeview Pines.

This mountain scenery was beautiful, and to an Oklahoma family coming from HOT summers, it was wonderfully cool. We often had short, quick afternoon showers to settle the dust, and there were no mosquitoes in those days, no snakes, and no poison ivy. My parents fell in love with the area in 1930 when we came to visit and made arrangements to buy their first 40 acres of land just south of B-9.

Since both my parents were schoolteachers, they had the summers off, and we began spending each summer in the mountains. Dad and several of his friends fixed up an old log cabin for us to stay in. Between 1932 and 1940, Dad built three more cabins, and in 1939 bought 40 more acres and repaired an old hand-hewn log home which had been built about 1917. I think the daughter of the man who built this log home is still living in California.

During our summers, many hours were spent hand digging wells and hand carrying pails of water to our cabin. We cut wood for the wood burning cook stove where Mother prepared our meals, baked all our bread, and heated water for dishwashing and bathing. We washed clothes on the washboard. Of course, we didn't have electricity or a telephone, so our summertime was spent in a much more primitive way than the modern accommodations we expect on a vacation today.

We depended on the local farming families for fresh milk, lettuce, and peas. We bought milk from the Dabovich family first. They lived north of County Road B-9 at the edge of the trees, and later we bought milk from the Coppy family who lived a little farther south and west of our land. Two of the younger girls carried a glass gallon jug of milk to us each evening from their farm. To keep our food fresh, we used ice boxes and had ice which had been cut from the lake in the wintertime and stored in sawdust in an icehouse. It was necessary to remember to empty the pan under the ice box each day, or you had a flood to mop.

To get the mail we walked the 1¼ miles each day to the highway to our mailbox, and packages would get very heavy on the return trip to our cabin. After my dad's retirement in the 1960s, he began modernizing our cabin and life became much simpler with electricity, running water, and indoor plumbing.

One of the families who lived a little farther to the north from the B-9 road, just into the trees, was a college professor, Dr. Thuringer, who came to the valley each summer. One year some of the horses and maybe the cows, too, became infected with sleeping sickness and my parents were very concerned so they sent back to Oklahoma for some vaccine for me. Dr. Thuringer was a research person, not an MD, but he had the necessary equipment and he agreed to give me the shots of vaccine. Mrs. Kaiser, a sister of Mrs. Thuringer, and her family visited the area and enjoyed it, too. They began coming as summertime residents.

Leo Arko and Joe Coppy can tell you many stories about the early farming families. Mrs. Coppy and Mrs. Necas were sisters, and they had a brother, Vencil Prohaska, and their mother who all lived in the area. Arko had a store on the next county road south of B-9 and Highway 64. I believe some of these families came to New Mexico to work in the coal mines near Raton, and they bought farming land in the Moreno Valley. The growing season was so short, they had trouble getting the crops to mature before frost. At one time, potatoes were a big crop, but they were affected with blight. Another year the farmers planted acres of peas, but the company they contracted with didn't get the pickers in before frost, so that whole crop failed.

As a city youngster spending the summers with the children of these families for playmates, I had a wonderful time hiking in the woods or visiting their farms while they were busy with chores. Our family's fourth generation still enjoys vacationing in the valley.

The Klondike and Payroll Mines

By Tracey Miller

In 1920 the mystique of the gold of the Moreno Valley was still alive. Fred W. Montague, Sr., of Chanute, Kansas, along with four other investors, acquired some land on Froelick Creek, on the lower slopes of Wheeler Peak at the end of State Highway 127, and incorporated as the Ideal Mining Company. They explored the area and opened three tunnels—Payroll #1, Payroll #2 and Klondike. The first two of these tunnels were little more than explorations, but the Klondike proved more valuable. Assay reports from the mine showed gold, silver, copper, and turquoise in very good amounts but the group, unfamiliar with mining and processing ore, hired an engineer from the Denver area who advised them to put in a mill. Only after the mill was built, shortly after 1920, did they discover that the grade of ore they were getting should have been smelted, and the nearest facility for ore smelting was Pueblo, Colorado.

The Klondike mining effort came to "a screeching halt" in 1926 when the discovery was made that the ore needed to be smelted, which meant trucking the ore to Pueblo, Colorado. At that point, the capital was virtually exhausted, and the quantity and quality of the ore was inadequate to justify continuing.

During the late 1920s and early 1930s getting people to invest in gold mining was extremely difficult; no one had money they wanted to invest. Mr. Montague, Sr., paid the resident caretaker of the mine out of his own pocket, believing that someone should oversee the mine, although it was defunct. The caretaker, Ed Wrigler, lived at the mine for many years until he died about 1940.

The sixteen cabins on the mining property were constructed prior to the mill and served as the mining office, a general store, the cook house, the residences of the owners (when in the area), and the residences of the miners. The original office building has been retained by the Montague family as their own summer cabin and has been remodeled for that purpose.

69

The maximum number of employees at the mine was about 13 during the summer, and of course most of them left, since winter there was extremely harsh, and mining was virtually impossible. Only the caretaker and the overseer stayed year-round. The other cabins on the property have been similarly refurbished to be used as summer homes. The Montague family has retained private ownership of the property and the use of the cabins.

The original owners were required by the state of New Mexico to hold a board of directors meeting on the premises once a year, so they gathered for that purpose annually. This practice continued until the 1940s when the present owner, Mrs. Fred W. Montague, Jr., drove her husband's parents out from Chanute, Kansas for the annual meeting.

Although there had been two very productive mines nearer Mt. Baldy, the Klondike mine, from its earliest days, was only marginally productive.

Exterior building of the Klondike Mine next to Idlewild. The mine was operational until the late 1920s. (photo by Elaine Jarzen)

The Ideal Mining Company was constantly issuing stock to gain additional working capital to push the tunnel farther into the mountain. Some of the two thousand small investors put as little as $10 into the venture. As the money from current investors was spent on the development of the mine, additional investors were sought.

Eventually the corporation failed to be able to continue the effort and became defunct. In 1972 at the time of the death of Mr. Fred W. Montague, Jr., his wife began the effort of reclaiming the title to the mine and lands. Since the corporation had been defunct for many years, people in the area seemed to think that the land was open to the public, though in fact it was not. After about seven years of legal efforts and considerable legal expenses, Mrs. Wynona Montague was able to gain title to the land around 1981.

A concern of the present owner is the danger to persons who might wander into the mill, which is not in good repair. In fact, some thought has been given to dismantling the old mill to eliminate the liability. The actual mine tunnel runs 1½ to 2 miles back into Mt. Wheeler and is not on the Montague property, but on the Moreno West Ranch. The entrance has been sealed. Trespassers, however, have tried to dig around the sealed entrance to create a new opening.

In more recent years, the Klondike mine area has served as a summer getaway for the Montague family and their friends——a cool, beautiful, retreat where one might see deer, elk, wild turkey, bear, bobcat, raccoon, porcupine, and even a red Mexican wolf. Although it was Mr. Montague Sr.'s idea to invest in a gold mine for his later years and for his children's benefit, having built his own security in oil, the mine never really provided the kind of income he and the other investors hoped for. Yet, as Wynona Montague points out, he really did leave his heirs a 'gold mine' in a way that he had not imagined. This acreage became for them a beautiful, restful, summer getaway, and it has provided that for four generations. The climate, the recreational opportunities, and the unparalleled beauty of the area draws the family back, along with a very different, more relaxed, and simpler lifestyle. Those, for the present-day residents, constitute the lure of the valley.

As of 1997, the cabins on the ten acres owned by the Montague family are leased to relatives and friends with the proviso that they will restore and maintain them and contribute to the maintenance of the owner's cabin. The miners built the original cabins and, at one point, a two-story hotel was planned for the area; today that foundation has been used to build another summer cabin.

Despite the fact that Idlewild developed adjacent to the mine in the 1930s, the only connections between Klondike and Idlewild are those of common interest and warm friendship.

Idlewild Community

Among the ranchers who took up land and raised cattle in the Moreno Valley of the late 19th and early 20th centuries was the Gallagher family. Charles Gallagher, born in 1882, married Mae Lowrey, the daughter of Joseph and Elizabeth Moore Lowrey, for whom Elizabethtown was named. Charles and Mae were married in 1908 in the Roman Catholic church in Therma (later named Eagle Nest). Even though they attended the same church, family tradition has it that Mae did not like Charles at first, "because he rode his horse into the saloons." Their 1,760-acre ranch included the land on which the Klondike mine lay, and it spread southeastward from the foothills of Wheeler Peak toward Therma and toward the Six Mile Ranch, owned by the W.S. Witt family.

In 1929, Charles Gallagher, according to family history, had a large herd of cattle being shipped to Kansas City precisely when the stock market began to fall. He had counted on $1,500 net cash out of the sale of the cattle, but because of market conditions, he actually received less than half that amount. As the family recalls, "Charlie lay on his bed all night without saying a word. He was just sick." As a result of that setback, and the need to sustain his own expenses on the ranch, he was forced to consider selling some of his land.

A genial cattle-buyer from the Texas panhandle, Thomas Cook, offered to buy 160 acres of choice timber land lying along the drainage of Froelick Creek from the Klondike Mine to near the ranch headquarters and the Gallagher home. He paid $10 per acre for the land which made up the $1,500 Gallagher needed plus a little extra. Cook wanted the land for his family to enjoy as a retreat, an "Idlewild," he said.

He built a small cabin near the western boundary of the acreage, near the road to the Klondike mine. Later he brought up his family and friends from the Texas Panhandle to his cool summer retreat, and the idea emerged of developing this "Idlewild." Two surveyors from Texas, Dave and Frank Stribling, were engaged to survey and plat the community. Lots 25 by 100 were laid out; sixteen lots to the block, with 20-foot easements resulting in 144 lots as building sites for future development as the Idlewild Community.

Mr. Dave Stribling became the caretaker, surveyor, and builder; he put a small cabin near Cook's, and this was later replaced by a larger home near the entrance of the Idlewild community. Following the death of Mr. Cook, his wife retained the land for many years before selling to Mr. Murphy of Albuquerque. It has since been sold again.

The task of marketing these lots was given to J.W. Dickerson, and he built a cabin on the southwest tract which became known as the Dickerson Division. His brother, Ray, also came up to assist with sales, and he built a cabin near the site of the present worship center. Lots sold in 1931 for $6, in 1934 for $16, in 1936 for $25, in 1960 for $50, in 1970 for $250 and in 1981 for $1,000.

The records kept by Mr. Cook show that in 1931 a dozen people purchased lots in Idlewild, and all but one of those buyers was from the Texas Panhandle; the lone exception, Judge Lohoy, was from Raton, New Mexico. The following year 87 people bought lots there, the vast majority, of them again from Texas; only seven were from New Mexico, and four from Oklahoma. The next year, 1933, an additional 86 persons bought land there; again, the vast majority of the buyers were from Texas, with a few from New Mexico and Oklahoma. Many of these original purchasers have kept their cabins and lots in the family, and it is not uncommon to find families who have been coming to Idlewild during the summers for four or even five generations. As of 1997 there were estimated to be 320 residential structures in the community, and the summer population, which fluctuates constantly, may go as high as 700.

A focal point of the community of Idlewild is the worship center—a place where people of all faiths come to worship together. According to many long-time residents, this shared experience has been the glue that has held the community together. There is no permanent minister, but individuals within the community take on the task of lining up speakers for the summer. Each visiting pastor is given a week's free vacation time in one of the cabins in exchange for his/her services, and in many cases, these visitors have been so enchanted by the area, they have eventually returned as property owners.

Special days are observed annually with "dinner on the grounds" and at these gatherings as many as 200 people may attend. The worship center, an open-air backdrop in the woods with an amphitheater-like setting, is generally in use each Sunday during the summer from June through Labor Day.

According to a history prepared by a committee of property owners in 1980, "The story of the worship center, its origin and growth, is an integral part of the history of the Idlewild community. The guiding spirit and influences which have welded the resort area into a community were fostered by the dedication of its citizens to the purpose set forth in the constitution. Mrs. Pearl Gould, with the assistance of several others, provided the leadership and inspiration in the beginning of the church services. In the early days, they started a Sunday School for the children of the community, holding it under the trees in a triangular plot in front of the Bratton cabin ... Rude wooden benches were provided by the men, a crude pulpit was fashioned from rough lumber, and attendance increased. Freewill offerings provided funds for the necessary equipment; eventually a portable field organ was purchased. Mrs. Buena Coleman of the mine area served as the faithful organist."

The Idlewild community does not have utilities except for electricity, which came in through the Kit Carson Electric Cooperative in the 1940s. Prior to that time kerosene lanterns or carbide miner's torches provided what light there was. Shortly after the introduction of electricity, LP gas became available and some of the residents installed gas heaters in their homes, though most continued to use wood for cooking and heating.

Water is provided by cisterns which collect rain and snow fall, and the bathrooms of most cabins are "a hot and cold running path."

By 1950 the community decided that it needed to incorporate as a nonprofit association "to contribute to the religious and the social welfare" of the community. On August 20, 1950, a meeting at Hardy Watson's was held for this purpose; a constitution and by-laws were drawn up and approved. In addition, a petition was drafted to the state of New Mexico for the purpose of incorporation. Seven trustees were elected to furnish leadership for the community, including: W.J. Becker, president, Mrs. Buena Coleman, secretary, and Mrs. Pearl Gould, treasurer. Members were Mr. Andy Wolverton, Rev. Don Harrell, Mr. Britt Marrs, and Mr. Nat Kaplan.

The by-laws of the community provided for only residential property; no businesses were permitted, and the sale of alcoholic beverages was strictly prohibited. Membership in the community was either active or honorary; property owners were active members, and honorary membership was granted only by the permission of the directors.

Nearby property owners could request honorary (non-voting) membership and be included in the religious and social activities of the community.

In the early '40s when Mr. Stribling retired, Mr. Cook sold all of his holdings except his home to Hardy Watson of Lawton, Oklahoma. A stucco building—his office and lodging—was built across the road from the caretaker's residence. Mayme and Britt Marrs were then installed as caretakers, and they continued in that capacity for nearly 50 years. The caretaker's residence was sold to Mr. Fancher Upshaw, Sr., who designated it as the permanent home of the Marrs so long as they lived and desired it. At that time, those property owners who wanted the protection and services offered by Britt and Mayme voluntarily began paying an annual fee of $12 each.

Today, recreation for the residents of the Idlewild Community is very different from the early days of the '30s. Then, the two gathering places for most people in the Moreno Valley were T.D. Neal's store in Eagle Nest or the American Legion Hall. But with the building of new roads and the increased availability of automobiles after World War II, the whole of northern New Mexico opened for them.

One property owner from Seattle, Washington, gave this statement: "I am in possession of an Abstract of Title, apparently executed in 1936 at the time my grandfather purchased the property. The first entry of the abstract indicated conveyance of '915 acres more or less' from the Board of Trustees of the Maxwell Land Grant company by Frank Springer, President, to Herman Froelick by Warranty Deed dated September 6, 1904. The abstract lists all recorded transactions and subdivisions of the original parcel up to 1936 when my grandfather purchased it (including the Dickerson subdivision)."

Thus, we understand that Charles Gallagher purchased his ranch lands from Herman Froelick in the early 1900s.

* * *

Tracy Miller, a resident of Angel Fire from December 1994, was the organizing pastor of the United Church of Angel Fire. In addition to his ordination, he holds a Ph.D. from the University of Tennessee in the field of English literature and language, and he has taught in numerous colleges in Tennessee, Kentucky, Oklahoma, and Colorado. He is also a published poet.

The Gallagher and Lowrey Families in the Moreno Valley

By Vicki Jameson

The story of these two pioneer families goes back to the year 1866, when gold was first discovered in the Moreno Valley. This find was instigated when a Ute Indian gave Captain John Moore of Fort Union, New Mexico a "hunk of pretty rock." The Indian led Captain Moore and his partner, William Kroenig, to the site where the rock had been found on the slopes of Baldy Mountain, elevation 12,549 feet. The "pretty rock" was rich in copper. Soon, gold was found in Willow Creek and by spring, 1867, a great number of miners had come to lay claims.

Captain William H. (John) Moore, born in County Cork, Ireland, moved his wife and daughter to the Moreno Valley. His wife, the former Matilden Smith, was born in Brookshire, Surrey, England. Moore had the area surveyed to plot a town, which he named Elizabethtown after his four-year-old daughter, Elizabeth, born at Ft. Union on April 4, 1863. Her father opened the first store in Elizabethtown.

Elizabeth became a beautiful dark-haired girl who taught Spanish in the town school and helped her mother run a boarding house. In 1880, she married Joseph Lowrey from Detroit, Michigan. The couple had nine children; two died in infancy and one girl died of measles on her 16th birthday. At the beginning of the 1900s, two of the Lowrey girls, Mae (16) and Bessy (14) sewed $10,000 worth of reported gold into their skirts to travel from Elizabethtown to Springer.

The Lowreys had a comfortable house with six bedrooms, a large living room, and fine furniture, including a piano. The Lowrey girls finished high school in Elizabethtown and attended business school in Trinidad.

The youngest Lowrey daughter, Maude, married a fellow named T.D. Neal. They had a son called Tal. Unfortunately, Maude died when their second child was born, and the baby also died. Later, Tal married a girl named Jeannine MacDougal. They had three children—two daughters and a son.

The landmark Eagle Nest Lodge. Ravaged by fire and now abandoned, it is located on the Walter Gant property. (photo by Elaine Jarzen)

Another Lowrey girl, Annie, married John Haddow. She was postmaster at the post office located in T.D. Neal's grocery store.

In 1868, another family arrived in the Moreno Valley to try their luck at mining in Elizabethtown. John Gallagher, from County Donegal, Ireland, married Mary McGarvey when he was twenty-five years old. She was fifteen. Gallagher had come to America to seek his fortune, or at least a better life. He had heard of the 1859 gold discovery in Colorado and the new discovery of gold in New Mexico after the Civil War in 1866. He decided this was the best place for him to try mining. 1868 was the first year the railroad came from Chicago to Cheyenne, Wyoming. Perhaps the Gallaghers traveled by train. Indians still sometimes attacked those who traveled in wagons because the white men were taking over their land.

The Gallaghers chose to settle on land a few miles from Elizabethtown because John wanted to have a ranch as well as be a miner. This land was a part of the original Maxwell Land Grant. As the years went by, the Gallaghers had a very large family of eight sons and two daughters (twins). The first son, Maurice, was born in 1876 or '77 and died at the age of fourteen. A later son was also named Maurice, a common practice in those times. Although two of the Gallagher's ten children died in childhood, several lived into their 80s and 90s. The birth and death dates of the Gallagher family members are taken from an old family bible, and they vary in two instances from the grave markers in a private Gallagher cemetery in Eagle Nest, New Mexico.

Elizabethtown was a boom town for ten to twelve years. Then the mining activity slowed down, with its first downturn occurring in 1875. The Gallagher ranch was located on land where the old white stone Lodge is near Eagle Nest Dam. In fact, part of the ranch house later became part of the Lodge. Sometime after John's death in 1905, Mary was forced to leave the ranch. The land was condemned in order to build Eagle Nest Dam. Mary contested but lost. She was paid a small amount of money for the ranch. Two other Irish families, the Duggans and the Graneys, were also forced to leave. After the dam was built, forming Eagle Nest Lake, the area became known as the town of Eagle Nest.

Charles Gallagher was the fifth son and by the time he was 23 years old, he had met Mae Lowrey from Elizabethtown. Charles Gallagher was a shy, tall, good-looking man with dark curly hair. He was two years older than Mae. She had known him for some time, but never liked him because, "he and his friends rode horses into saloons." Eventually, she decided he wasn't too bad, and she agreed to join a group of young people and go with him to a dance in Red River. This would be a 12-mile horseback ride. After the dance, they had breakfast and returned to E'Town as soon as the sun rose.

After two years of courting, they were married in 1908. Charles opened a butcher shop in Cimarron. Mae, who graduated from high school and attended business school in Trinidad, kept the books. But Charlie's dream had always been to have a ranch. They moved back to a homestead in the Moreno Valley. Charles and Mae had three sons, Edward, William (Bill) and Charles. Charles, Jr. was tall like his father. The boys rode horses, plowed, planted grass, weeded the garden, mended fences, and took tourists to Blue Lake.

Ranchers came from as far as 100 miles away to go to dances which lasted until dawn. Mae liked waltzes and quadrilles best. In 1922, Charles bought a Dodge pickup for himself and bought Mae a Buick. Things were going well. Charlie sent a load of cattle to Kansas and was promised $1,500. But the Depression of the thirties had hit, and he received only $700. The original ranch acreage was reduced to 1760 acres when Charlie sold some of the best timber land for $10 an acre. This area later became known as Idlewild.

After graduating from Raton High School, Bill Gallagher attended New Mexico State University before transferring to Colorado State University in Fort Collins. Halfway into his junior year, the Japanese attacked Pearl Harbor, and Bill left school to join the U.S. Army Air Corps. He served four years in the Asian Pacific and was assigned to an air-sea rescue squadron in the Aleutian Islands. He was honorably discharged in 1946. He returned to the Moreno Valley to help his parents, Mae and Charlie Gallagher, run the family ranch.

In 1948, Bill married Laurelle Robin Errington at St. Mel's Catholic Church in Eagle Nest. They lived only a quarter mile from his parents' ranch. For a total of 27 years. Charlie and Bill raised cows and calves, and planted wheat and alfalfa. After Charlie died in 1967, Bill's mother, Mae, joined her sons in partnership of the ranch. They decided not to run cattle, but to lease the land. During the summers from 1959 to 1979, Bill and his cousin, Tal Neal, ran the fishing at Eagle Nest Lake.

Bill Gallagher instilled in his family a strong sense of public service during his lifetime. In 1952, Bill was elected to the Colfax County Commission, a position held earlier by his father. In 1956, he was elected to the New Mexico State Senate, serving three consecutive terms, and holding the position of Majority Floor Leader. Later, he served on the New Mexico State Fair Board and the New Mexico State Racing Commission. He returned to the County Commission for a four-year term in 1969. During the '70s and '80s, he served on the Board of Directors and as Chairman of Western Production Credit Association. In 1979, he joined Angel Fire Corporation as purchasing agent, continuing until his retirement in 1986. Between 1979 and 1984 he served as co-publisher of the *Sangre de Cristo Chronicle.*

Bill Gallagher died in October 1988 at the age of 67, in Raton. His wife, Laurelle, stayed at the home ranch west of Eagle Nest. Bill was buried there.

Bill and Laurelle's son, Joseph, was born in Raton, New Mexico, December 15, 1949. Joe attended grade school in Eagle Nest, some in Raton and some at St. Francis School in Santa Fe. He was a page in the New Mexico Senate in Santa Fe. He attended high school at Holy Cross Abbey Preparatory School in Canon City, Colorado. Although he was reluctant to leave home to go to the Abbey, after four years, he was sad to leave the Abbey. He received his College Preparatory Diploma in 1967. He spent four summers as a fishing guide on Eagle Nest Lake.

In 1967, Joe received some very sad news. He lost his beloved grandfather in November. He had spent a great deal of time with his grandparents. They taught him many things including how to play bridge, patch, and poker. His grandfather insisted that he learn to cook. He thought all men should have this skill. When Joe visited them, it was his turn to cook on Tuesdays. His grandparents were great story tellers. He also learned about gardening from them, and this is still one of his interests. His grandmother lived to be almost one hundred years old. She died in January 1986.

By this time, Joe was in college. He received his B.S. Cum Laude in English American Studies from the University of New Mexico in Albuquerque in 1971. He received a M.A. degree in Anglo-Irish Studies at the National University of Ireland in Dublin. He worked as Associate Editor of the Great Western Publishing Co. in Temecula, California, from 1972-73, editing and publishing *Angel Fire Life* and *Baca Grande Life*, newspapers of land developers Arizona Land and Cattle Co. (AZL). The first copies were printed in Riverside and Hemet, California. Joe brought 20,000 copies of each paper to New Mexico in a U-Haul truck. He did articles on new people moving into the Angel Fire and Baca Grande, Colorado areas, as well as writing news and providing property owners information for these new developments. He continued to publish these newspapers until January 1974.

Joe returned to the Moreno Valley in 1973 to write "The Legend of Angel Fire." He also worked from March until the middle of May to start two other newspapers, the *Moreno Valley Lantern,* and the *Red River Prospector.* They contained news stories, special feature articles, editorials, and advertising.

He set up an office in a family ranch-owned cabin near his parents' home. He had a card table and a portable typewriter. Joe laid out the articles, photographs and advertising for the monthly newspapers which were printed in Alamosa, Colorado. The papers were then brought back to Eagle Nest and separated by Joe and Eagle Nest Postmaster "Sonny" Johnson into zip code packets for mailing to subscribers. Additional copies were distributed locally. The first issues came out the July 4th weekend of 1973, and these publications continued until February 1975, when Joe combined the two newspapers into the *Sangre de Cristo Chronicle.*

During these years, he became good friends with Glen Miller and "Bits" Hoover. They had a continuing bridge or gin game going on in the 19th Hole at the Country Club. He considered Glen Miller to be his mentor. Glen Miller and Bill Miller were investors in Angel Fire with Roy H. and G.F. LeBus who started the development in the early '60s. The first ski slopes were cut in 1962 and opened in 1965. They later sold the development to AZL. Some of the LeBus family still live in the valley.

Kay and Russ Sylvester were very good friends of Joe and his parents. Every Friday afternoon, Joe would go skiing in Red River. During this time, he was considering making a change in his life. He decided to leave Angel Fire because he missed living in a city, traveling, and the arts available in a large city. By this time, he was past his 29th birthday and found that trying to work when everyone else was on vacation or retired was difficult. Max and Nancy Mertz were influential in his moving to Houston. Also, his great aunt and uncle lived there.

Another factor in Joe's choice was that he had an interest in geology and Houston was a boom town in the oil industry. He worked for PennWell Publishing Company for five years from 1979-84, holding the positions of Editor for *Electronic Rig Stats/Worldwide Offshore Rigfinder*, and of Assistant Editor of *Ocean Oil Weekly Report, Offshore Magazine*. From 1984 to the present time, he has been with Petroconsultants Inc. in Houston, as Editor of "Petroconsultants International Oil Letter."

He is active in community and civic associations, such as Business Volunteers for the Arts-Houston, The Alley Theatre, and Theatre Lab Houston. His sister, Lori, also lives in Houston where she practices law. His other sister, Ngiare, lives in Clayton, New Mexico, and has two children. Joe (Jay, as he is called in Houston) will probably have a home in the Moreno Valley in his retirement. He enjoys coming to visit and is proud of his heritage.

It is interesting to note that Joe's great-great-grandfather Moore and his great-grandfather Gallagher came to the Moreno Valley in the quest for gold. Now Joe's career is in a business related to the quest for oil. The fact that Charles Gallagher married Mae Lowrey, and Tal Neal married Maude Lowrey, made their children cousins. It also meant that Elizabeth Moore Lowrey was their great-grandmother, tying the two families together.

* * *

Viola (Vicki) Shaeffer Jameson was born in Central City, Colorado. She majored in Nursing at E.O.C. of Ed. in Oregon and Pharmacy at C.U. She and her husband, Jamie, have two sons and two daughters and seven grandchildren. She was very interested in writing about the Gallagher and Lowrey families because she grew up in a gold mining town where five generations of her family lived from 1868-1942.

The Gallagher and Lowrey Family Tree

Great-Great Grandparents
Capt. William H. (John) Moore
Born County Cork, Ireland
Died 5-1-1873
Rayado Creek, Colfax County, NM
Married Matilden Smith, Born 1846
Brookshire, Surrey, England

Gallagher Family

Great Grandfather
John Gallagher
Born 1843
Ballyshannon Co., Donegal, Ireland
Died 5-25-1905 Moreno Valley

Great Grandmother
Mary McGarven
Born 1853
Died 1916

Grandfather
Charles Gallagher
Born 3-1883, Moreno Valley
Married 1908
Died 11-1967, Raton, NM

Grandmother
Mae Lillian Lowrey
Born 6-8-1886, Elizabethtown
Died 1-16-1986, Clayton, NM

Father
William Clyde Gallagher
Born 4-20-1921, Cimarron, NM
Married 2-19-1948, Eagle Nest, NM
Died 10-9-1988, Raton, NM

Mother
Laurelle Robin Errington
Born 7-12-29, Raton, NM

Joseph Charles Gallagher
Born 12-15-49, Raton, NM
Ngiare A. McNaughten
Lori M. Gallagher

Lowrey Family

Great Grandfather
Joseph Lowrey
Born 4-6-1840, Detroit, MI
Married 6-20-1880
Died 1913

Great Grandmother
Elizabeth Catherine Moore
Born 4-4-1863, Ft. Union, NM
Died 12-20-1934, Eagle Nest, NM

Grandfather
Talmage De Witt Neal
Born 4-1890, Stroud, Okla
Died 7-1953, Albuquerque, NM

Grandmother
Maude Lowrey
Born Elizabethtown
Died Trinidad

Father
Talmage Dennis Neal
Born 1-16-1923, Trinidad
Died 2-7-1992, Raton

Mother
Jeannine MacDougal
Born 8-20-30, Raton, NM

Laura Lynn Neal Shields
Talmage Dirk Neal
Kimberly Lane Perino

Val Verde Ranch

by Elaine V. Sandberg-Jarzen

This 800-acre ranch is located off Highway 64 behind the Vietnam Veterans National Memorial in Angel Fire, New Mexico. After the turn of the century, a ranch house was built by a family who raised cattle and wheat. The rancher's young daughter became pregnant by one of the hired hands. Her parents, shamed by their daughter's condition, locked her in the basement until the child was born. According to oral tradition, she and her baby both died during childbirth and were buried in Elizabethtown's cemetery. People who have inhabited the residence since these unfortunate deaths, are convinced that the young girl's ghost still lives there. The structure today is referred to as the "Hip" house due to the unique pitch and style of its roof.

In the roaring 1920s, a spacious lodge, known as the "Ice Palace," was built. The enterprising owner opened a gambling saloon that catered to the rich and famous. Two notorious Chicago gang members, "Pretty Boy Floyd" and "Baby Face Nelson," frequented the establishment. They took the train to Raton, then traveled westward to the Val Verde Ranch for a wild and wooly getaway. The legendary poker table spanned the length of the entire gambling hall. When high rollers wanted to fill their empty bellies with food or drink a shot of whiskey, they would summon the servants by pressing a buzzer underneath the table.

Historical accounts of Val Verde Ranch jump four decades from the 1920s until 1966, when Dr. Victor Westphall purchased the property from Mr. Charles Balduini of Albuquerque. Victor opened up a small ski area on the property. He cleared trees for an easy beginner's slope and installed a rope tow. Two additional runs were added, along with a poma lift. Victor also designed a golf course and laid $30,000 worth of grass seed for 9 holes, which would eventually be expanded to 18 holes.

Dr. Westphall's plans for developing the area came to an abrupt halt when his son David was killed in Vietnam in 1968. Unable to continue with the project, he sold the ranch to three investors: Mr. Crawford, a dentist, Mr.

Phillips, an attorney, and Mr. Senter, a mobile home distributor. A strange coincidence occurred. Mr. Senter insisted that the closing papers be signed on May 22, 1969, which happened to be the exact date of David's death one year later. Misfortune struck once again. Shortly after the new partners took over operations, Mr. Senter and his family perished in a plane crash on their way to New Mexico.

The surviving owners quickly sold the ranch to a group called the Religious Order of Spectrum. For a number of years, church groups would gather at Val Verde, enjoying ski vacations that included room and board. When the Spectrum's non-profit status changed, they sold the ranch to Betty Fleissner of Eagle Nest. The historical "Hip" House and "Ice Palace" lodge were scheduled to be torn down by the end of 1996.

Interior of the "Ice Palace" on the Val Verde Ranch, a gambling hall frequented by high-rolling gangsters. Photo taken shortly before the building was to be demolished. (Photo by Elaine Jarzen)

The Six Mile Ranch

by Tracey Miller

Not all of those in the Moreno Valley were miners, business people, or outlaws; there were some excellent ranches and farms in the valley. In 1860 Wilford Barton Witt, who had grown up near Charleston, Tennessee and had married Nancy Ann King in 1843, left his wife and four children in Arkansas. He headed west alone and was not seen by the family for 20 years.

He homesteaded land in the Moreno Valley, and over time he bought up other homesteads until he developed a large and well-stocked ranch. This ranch was on Six Mile Creek (six miles south of where E'town would be). The story of how he was reunited with his family was recounted by his grandson, Walter Scott, in an interview for a historical piece on Taos.

Walter told this story: "The Witts back in Arkansas lost track of their father, for mails were uncertain ninety-six years ago—perhaps he did not write. His son, William Sim Witt, grew up and went to Colorado, ran into a man who said he had met a man in Taos by the name of Witt. Could this be his long-lost father? Should he go to Taos? If he did not go, would he forever wonder and regret? He'd better go. He went—and the fellow in Taos *was* his father!"

In 1872, William Sim Witt bought his father's ranch and brought out his wife, Nancy Scribner Witt, and their three children—Lee, Julia (who later married John Dunn) and Lizzie. Fanny, Clara, Minnie, and Walter were born and raised in the Moreno Valley. Although family records do not reflect the sale, the *Elizabethtown Souvenir* says, "The ranch was settled upon in 1865 by its present owner, and was later sold to a gentleman named Hunt, from whose hands it passed into the possession of W.H. King and W.S. Witt, and then into the hands of the present owner." That present owner is identified at the top of that page as Mrs. Nancy Witt. According to the family, the ranch was passed from Wilford Barton Witt to his wife Nancy in 1881 and subsequently to their son, William Simeon Witt (called Sim by the family).

William Henry King, the brother of Barton's wife and an educated man, had gone to the California gold fields with the '49ers. He fought through the Civil War and ended with the rank of Colonel in the Confederate States of America. After the war, he joined his nephew in the Moreno Valley and continued to work with Barton for many years.

In addition to the ranch business, Barton and "great Uncle King," as he came to be known to the children and grandchildren of Barton and Nancy, also built a sawmill which was entirely under roof. This enormous, shingled building was built on a hillside and was constructed of large, sawed timbers with a causeway leading into the mill. With this facility they could saw lumber from early spring to late fall. The mill not only provided posts for fencing, timbers, planks, and shingles; it provided the materials for the Six Mile Ranch house. The house had walls 6 to 8 inches thick with shingles on the outside and the space between the interior and exterior walls was filled with sawdust for insulation. Other ranches were established about this time as well, notably the Mountain View Ranch, near Bobcat Pass, and the Gallagher Ranch which lay adjacent to the Six-Mile on the north.

Mr. W.S. Witt's sawmill business supplied wood to the miners and the businesspeople in E'town. The adobe ruins south of E'town on Moreno Creek are the remains of one of his mills. His mill business took him away from the Six-Mile Ranch at busy times of the year, and Nancy Witt took over that responsibility. It may be the frequent absences of Sim that caused some to conclude that Nancy was widowed, as the reference to "Mrs. Witt, a widow," in the account of the Blackjack Ketchum gang indicates. Sim, however, lived until 1917. Sim and Nancy had eight children: three boys (Lee, Lewis, and Walter Scott) and five girls (Julia, Mary Elizabeth, Minnie, Fanny Louise and Clara Alice). The management of the ranch passed from Nancy Witt to Walter Scott Witt (born 1885), the sixth of their eight children.

The Six Mile Ranch contained over a thousand acres, and it provided pasturage for the Hereford cattle that had been brought in by W.H. King and Wilford Barton Witt. Nancy Witt, however, gave the ranch a distinction when she bought heifers instead of steers which would be fattened and sold off each year. By converting to heifers, she increased the numbers of her herd and sold off the young steers to other ranchers who were fattening cattle during the summer. Of course, this procedure also meant that she had to see her heifers through some hard winters, and she had to help with calving. Because of this creative approach, the ranch was often referred to as "the heifer ranch."

Sim and Nancy Witt were both hard workers; Nancy, in addition to her ranch work, had a large vegetable garden, milk cows, chickens, and fields of potatoes, which she traded for wheat for the chicken feed. Also, the wheat was ground into flour at the Old Taos flour mill at Ranchos de Taos. On the ranch were three essential buildings: the cellar which contained heads of cabbage, turnips, onions, carrots, beets, potatoes, and bins of apples; the smokehouse with cured hams and bacon, barrels of corn beef, and kegs of sauerkraut; and the adobe milk house where a frozen beef would hang all winter and large crocks of butter were stored.

During the summer there were three months of school in the Moreno Valley; the school building was about two miles south of the ranch. In winter, however, when the sawmill was closed, Sim and Nancy took their children to Taos and put them in public school there. In 1889 or '90, Nancy had a school built on the ranch and Great Uncle King taught them. Little Walter Scott Witt, born in 1885 and too young to go to school at the time, was very angry at being excluded, so he would throw rocks at the building in protest. Later, Uncle King was replaced by young women who were hired to teach at the school and who lived at the ranch.

If this ranch life seemed like long hours of boring work and little recreation, one has to remember that there were trips into E'Town, Taos, and Therma for supplies and for fun and dancing. In fact, dances were also held at Arko's dance hall farther south in the valley near what is now County Road B-8.

These dances would draw people from all over the valley as far south as Black Lake, and the dances would sometimes last throughout the weekend. If a priest or a circuit riding minister happened to be there on a Sunday morning, there might be a Catholic mass or a service held in the dancehall. In fact, according to its pamphlet, St. Mel's Catholic Church in Eagle Nest cites in its history the existence of this Roman Catholic community, long before a church was built. "Services were held in Arko's dance hall for a number of years, until a church was built in 1936."

Kay Witt Potvin recalled, "We all were musical; my dad (Walter Scott Witt) played the violin; my brother Ray played the accordion and concertina; my brother Sam played the five-string banjo and mandolin, and I played the piano." Kay recalled that the dances lasted the entire weekend; people did not sleep, they danced, but they did stop for meals, and usually Mrs. Arko would serve all those present. While reflecting upon her family's musical background, Mrs. Potvin paused to get out her father's violin, a beautifully aged and well-worn instrument. She said, "If you will look inside the box of the violin, you'll see the name and age of the man who made it." Inside the instrument was burned the phrase "Guarnerius facit cremoni, anno 1725." Presumably, this had to be done prior to the gluing of the back onto the sides of the music box. Whether this represents an authentic Guarnerius, or a commercial reproduction of his work, this writer has not determined, but the instrument was at least 100 years old according to the Witt family records.

Among the stories told by and about Walter Scott Witt, who died in 1949 at the age of 64, is one about his contracting to deliver wild horses to be shipped to St. Louis. In 1909 the Moreno Valley was considered "open range"—there were open, rolling parks and woodlands where horses roamed freely, and whoever could catch them could have them. Walter used two different methods of catching the wild horses. The first involved releasing a herd of domesticated horses in a park. The wranglers would find the trail of a wild stallion and his band of six or eight mares and drive them toward the gentle herd. Blending the wild horses with the gentle ones enabled them to corral the whole herd. Then the gentle horses were released again, and the wild ones confined until they had a herd of 200 head of wild horses. These were then driven to the railhead at Ute Park to be shipped back East for $7 per head.

The second method of catching the wild ones was used especially for wiser wild ones that had been previously tamed but had gone wild again. They were especially leery of humans and harder to catch. Finding a trail of the wild ones, the wranglers would build a concealed trap corral across the trail, deep in a wooded area. When the wild ones followed the trail, they would be driven at top speed into the trap and the trap gate, concealed from the herd, would be closed quickly by the cowboys. Often these "soured" horses required some extreme measures to control them. Sometimes cowboys had to tie the horse's front leg to its tail; if the horse fought too hard, he would throw himself.

Another story about Walter Scott Witt's adventures was about his ride from the Moreno Valley to Taos when he was told of the birth of his daughter, Katherine, in 1919.

The family's pattern had been to move the family to Taos during the winter so that the children could attend school. In 1895, William Sim Witt moved to Taos and purchased the San Geronimo Lodge where he settled and where his grandchildren came to spend the winter. It was there that Walter Scott's wife, Della Mae Phipps Witt, gave birth to Katherine. Walter Scott was still up on the ranch trying to get the cattle through the harsh winter when he received the news that the child had come, so he immediately saddled a horse and began the 28-mile ride over the mountain and down the Taos Canyon in very deep snow. The road in those days lay north of the present Palo Flechado Pass on U.S. Highway 64, and it was a steep, narrow wagon road. Though it took a day of fighting the drifts, Walter Scott got to the Lodge as soon as he could to see his new daughter.

Besides those who were ranching, a number of the homesteaders were farmers, and their names are well-known to the families of the first residents of the Valley—-Arko, Dabovich, Andreolli, and others. These families homesteaded in the area and began to raise those hardy vegetables which would prosper in the high cold climate of the Moreno Valley.

Apparently around the beginning of World War I, several of these families from Central and Eastern Europe came to the American West to avoid the violence that was breaking out. Correspondence received includes the following: "My father, Dan Mellaragno and family of Italian descent, moved to the Moreno Valley in 1915 or 1916. They bought 40 acres for $10.00 per acre, and a lot of hard work went into clearing the land. First a cellar was built and later on a house of timbers, of which each timber was hand-hewn with an axe. The ground was broken by horse and plow, and the crops—potatoes, grain, oats, barley, and wheat—grew very tall. The land was paid for by the crops we raised. But the winters were harsh. All the school children walked to school, sometimes through four or five feet of snow. There were 20 or 30 pupils and one teacher taught up to the sixth grade. Dances and school plays were the highlights of the community activities."

The history of the Leo Arko family in the Moreno Valley goes back to 1917, when Leo Arko, Sr. (1884-1962) came into the valley. Leo, Jr. told how his family came up through what was later to become Eagle Nest Lake when they first entered the Valley. At the time (1917), this low-lying area near the mouth of the canyon was a large and fertile hay meadow.

Arko had been a coal miner at Dawson, near Colfax, New Mexico, after immigrating from Yugoslavia. He continued to return to Dawson to work in the mines when times were hard and income in the Valley was scarce. The family settled about one-half mile west of the present family home on county road B-8, and that is where Leo Arko, Jr. was born in 1923. According to Mr. Arko, Jr., he had an older brother who was also named Leo, Jr., but the brother was killed at an early age when the family's still exploded. And so, when the next son was born, he was given the name Leo, Jr. to maintain the family tradition. There were 14 children born to Leo, Sr. and his wife; the 13th was Leo, Jr.

Leo, Jr. attended the Moreno Valley School which was located about one mile south of county road B-8 on Highway 64, but the two-story building burned in 1952. The school had one teacher for each two or three grades when he attended there. He recalls seeing stuffed eagles decorating the hallway. When he was about 12 years old, he began to work on the farm, plowing with either a two-horse or a four-horse hitch. The time he had for recreation was spent in fishing, hunting, tramping about in the woods, or ice-skating. He reports that most of the people he knew when growing up were homesteaders and farmers with farms of 40-80 acres. These farms produced large quantities of peas, lettuce, cabbages, and potatoes, which were taken by wagon to the sorting shed in Ute Park where the railroad ended. The produce then was shipped by rail to the processing plants.

Leo, Jr. recalls cutting blocks of ice off the lake and storing it in an underground "ice house," where it was packed in snow and straw or sawdust from his brother's sawmill in Eagle Nest. He remembers the store at Agua Fria, which had a post office, and was run by a family named Reilly. During World War II he was gone from the valley for three years and later spent four years in Oklahoma before returning. His mother served as a midwife, since there was no doctor available then, unless one were willing and able to make the trip to Taos, Dawson, or Raton—and those were all-day trips.

He recalls a winter in the '30s when the snow was especially heavy and there was no mail in the valley for a week.

Abundant lettuce crop in the 1950s

Eagle Nest, New Mexico

By Jo Bynum

In the days before Spaniards occupied New Mexico, various Native American tribes freely roamed the bottom of the Moreno Valley along the Cimarron River in search of golden eagle feathers used for ceremonial worship. Later, as mountain men entered the valley, they were attracted to the Cimarron River by the beaver population, extracting a goodly amount despite the Spanish dictates against trapping in New Mexico streams. In 1841 the area became part of the 1,714,764 acre Maxwell Land Grant.

During the mid to late 1800s, the lower area of the Moreno Valley south of the then-prominent Elizabethtown was open ranch land. In the early 1900s that face began to change dramatically.

The Pobar Family Tragedy

During the early 1900s George and Margaret Pobar emigrated from Yugoslavia to New Mexico. As ranchers and dairy farmers, they did well for themselves and soon had a home in Raton, a winter ranch in Maxwell and, by 1917, a summer ranch in the Moreno Valley that is now part of the Gorman ranch. In fact, one of the peaks north of the Gorman ranch and just below Wheeler Peak is named Pobar Peak after the family.

The Pobars worked the ranches with their eleven children and raised wheat, barley, oats, potatoes, cabbage, and lettuce. According to George's son, Joseph, iceberg lettuce originated in the Moreno Valley and the Pobars, Witts and Gormans were the first to grow it. Joseph also said he recently found records that his father sold the barley raised to the Coors Brewery in Golden, Colorado.

Being of generous spirit, George Pobar would load unsold dairy products into a wagon and take them to the mining towns of Elizabethtown, Sugarite, and Dawson to give to the poor who couldn't afford to buy his products. He was known throughout the area for his strong will and generosity.

Joseph was born in 1920 and lived the first years of his life during Prohibition (1920-1933). According to Joseph, a still was located in the canyon of the property his parents took over. FBI officials, referred to as deputies at that time, came in and blew up the still when he was four or five years old. For the next several years these deputies played a large role in the life of the Pobars.

Sometime in the late 1920s one of the deputies, Ray Sutton, disappeared. Sutton's car was found in a ravine on Pobar property near Dawson, buried under leaves and covered by the trees. The driver's seat and running board were covered with blood, but there was no body. The Pobar family helped in the massive search effort, but the body was never discovered. According to Joseph, the FBI tried to pin the murder on his dad, George Pobar, because of suspected bootlegging.

During the early 1930s, the deputies showed up at the Pobar home, still asking questions about where to find Sutton's body. No Trespassing signs had been posted on all the fences and gates, and since the deputies showed no warrant, George Pobar met them at the gate with his shotgun telling them to "get the hell off my land."

Three months later, Joseph and his older brother, John, found their dad shot dead in the middle of the road on their property. The boys ran to the nearest neighbors, the Witts, who drove all the way to Therma to make the call to the police.

Joseph said the detectives who came to investigate the case couldn't find out who had murdered George Pobar, so they accused the two boys, Joe and John. Evidence was withheld at the boys' hearing and some of the evidence presented did not match up with the crime scene. The boys' mother, Margaret, held to the belief, and voiced it to the judge, that her husband had been killed by the FBI because he could not tell them where Sutton's body was.

Soon word spread throughout Colfax County that the boys were to be tried for the murder of their father and, if convicted, would get 50 to 60 years in prison. George Pobar and his family had built a good reputation in the county, so the court could not find enough people to sit on a jury for the trial.

Even though the case never went to court, the news media of the time declared the boys guilty. To hush things up, the judge decided that the best thing to do was send the older boy, John, to Father Flanagan at Boys Town, Nebraska. John went to Boys Town where he finished high school before joining the Navy to fight in World War II.

Margaret Pobar leased out the ranch land in the Moreno Valley while her sons were away at war. When they came home, the boys were not interested in farming or ranching and went looking for other occupations. When all the sons and daughters had come of age and found other occupations for their lives, Margaret sold the ranch to Gene Wilson. The property eventually became part of the Gorman ranch.

Joseph Pobar moved to Denver with his wife. They raised eight children—four sons and four daughters—and have 14 grandchildren. All of the children and their families live in the Denver area around Aurora and Parker.

Joe's wife died a few years ago and, after 50 years away, he decided it was time to come home. He moved back into the house his parents had built 80 years earlier in Raton. His daughter, Margaret, also moved to Raton and was the contact who first brought this story to the attention of this writer.

According to Margaret, her uncle John lives in Colorado and, due to the humiliation he suffered surrounding his father's death, refuses to set foot in New Mexico.

Eagle Nest Dam

Ranchers Charles and Frank Springer and the Cimarron Valley Land Company were granted a permit (Permit #71) in 1907 to impound the water of the Cimarron River for irrigation by building a dam. Construction on the dam began in 1916 and continued through 1918.

The dam created a 100,000 acre-foot reservoir called Eagle Nest Lake.

Springer stocked the lake with trout, and fishermen began to arrive. With the fishermen came the entrepreneurs who were able to envision what Eagle Nest would become. One of the earliest of these was T. D. Neal, frequently referred to as the founding father of Eagle Nest.

T. D. Neal

T. D. Neal was a man of small stature with a pioneer spirit and the determination to realize his dreams. Around 1919 he arrived in the Moreno Valley from Stroud, Oklahoma. With him were his foster father, H. J. Johnson, and his brother, Roy.

These three men envisioned the prosperity of the Moreno Valley. When they arrived, the only building in the area known as Eagle Nest was the "old Beimer shack." T. D. bought land, platted the town, and had it surveyed. By the spring of 1920, construction of T. D. Mercantile, the first large building and business establishment, was completed.

Mining was on the decline in Elizabethtown as T. D. and H. J. began to set up shop. T. D. bet his partner that the store would gross $10,000 in the first year—T. D. won the bet. Their labor was rewarded as the area became an increasingly popular haven for Texans wishing to escape the stresses of work and the heat of summer. Word spread and other businesses soon began to arrive.

Earnest and Charlie Bukove built the Valley Garage in 1923 on the site where the Gold Pan now stands. They also built the Valley Store on the south side of the road across from the garage. This pushed T. D. to expand his one-room store by adding a garage and the first cabins in town.

When the population finally shifted from Elizabethtown to this beautiful spot by the lake, T.D. petitioned for a post office. The petition was granted, and the town finally had a name—Therma, after a relative of the postal inspector. The name didn't stick and, in 1935, after mail addressed to Eagle Nest Lake flooded in, village residents decided to rename their town Eagle Nest.

As success set in and profits increased, T. D. built his own home on the main street. The white and green-trimmed house stood in the center of the village and, in 2021, is the location of Enchanted Eagle Park. T. D. married one of the valley beauties, Maude Lowrey, daughter of Elizabethtown-namesake, Elizabeth Moore Lowrey. Until their son, Talmage (Tal) Dennis Neal was born January 16, 1923, Maude helped T. D. in the store and post office. Maude died in 1931 when Tal was eight years old.

Wanting to bring people to Eagle Nest and see it prosper, T. D. instituted the Eagle Nest Fish Fry. He contracted the catching of fish, iced them down, and supplied the wood and coffee at no charge for 2,000 to 3,000 people. With cars lined up for miles from the old Eagle Nest Lodge to the Cloverleaf Motel, 1936 was one of the fish fry's best years.

T. D.'s vision was large, and he welcomed a challenge. His desire to turn nothing into something led him to numerous business ventures. He built a store in Agua Fria (where the blinking light at highways 64 and 434 is today) and installed a post office. In 1945, when the Maxwell Land Grant was dispersed, he had the opportunity to buy land around Agua Fria for $12 an acre. According to T. D.'s son, Tal—who sold land in Angel Fire during the late 1970s for $12,000 an acre—his dad refused the offer because it was "too damn high."

He was again partnered with H. J. in the ownership of a store in Red River and he bought a 320-acre ranch at the head of Red River where he raised Hereford cattle.

Ranching may have been one of T. D.'s favorite activities. He fully participated in the various aspects of the business, enjoying the big cattle drives, the branding and the shipping. His brood cows proved to have such

The year 1989 brought 89 inches of snow during one storm in early February. After facing the deluge of controversy during the gambling years, a little snow left the Laguna Vista undaunted. (Photo printed with permission of the *Sangre de Cristo Chronicle*)

a high milk capacity that on long drives up from the winter pastures in Ute Park the cows had to be tied to trees and milked—the calves could not drink enough.

Until the mid-1950s when modern refrigeration arrived in the area, a "winter harvest" took place at Eagle Nest during the dead of winter each year. A truck was driven to the spot where the ice harvest would take place and loaded with blocks of ice cut from the frozen lake. The ice was stored in sawdust at Eagle Nest Dam headquarters, T. D. Mercantile, and several other Eagle Nest locations. This ice was the only means of keeping drinks, food, and catches of fish fresh during the summer months.

Besides being involved in town politics, T. D. organized a delegation to go to Santa Fe to convince the powers-that-be to route Highway 64 through Eagle Nest. In addition to his various business ventures, T. D. enjoyed the other "social" activities—poker, horse racing, and fishing—that Eagle Nest had to offer in the 1930s and 1940s.

T. D. died of a massive stroke in the summer of 1953 just days after riding up to some of the high lakes near Wheeler Peak to check his cattle. Feeling ill after returning from the trip and taking into account his history of high blood pressure, T. D. left for Albuquerque to seek medical help and never returned to the Moreno Valley.

Eagle Nest Gambling Days

Even though it was illegal in New Mexico, gambling hit its peak by the mid to late 1930s. Big-time gamblers were running the circuit between Las Vegas and Eagle Nest, sleeping all day and playing all night with stakes in the tens of thousands of dollars. Old-timers refer to that period as a time when "you did anything you were big enough to do." Evidently some of the Eagle Nest residents were pretty big!

Many of the stores in Eagle Nest had slot machines, while Julio's, Gold Pan, El Monte Hotel (now the Laguna Vista), and Eagle Nest Lodge featured roulette wheels and gaming tables as well. According to some of the old-timers, the games were rigged—the ball on the roulette table could be stopped by a row of buttons at the back, mercury spots doctored the dice, and the cards were marked.

El Monte took entertainment a step further by providing ladies of the evening accessible only by a hidden staircase.

Eagle Nest was a rough place during those days. It is said that disputes between rivals—whether businesses or individuals—often ended with bullets being volleyed back and forth across the main street from roofs of prominent establishments.

The 1940s saw the end of open gambling in Eagle Nest. The police were ordered to destroy all signs of gambling in the village. Slot machines were hacked to pieces in the streets. According to stories circulating through the area, some of the proprietors got wind of the bust and dumped slot machines into the lake to avoid prosecution. Gambling retired to back rooms where bootleg slot machines were still in use.

Eagle Nest Post Office

After her sister Maude's death around 1931, Annie Lowrey Haddow and her husband John moved closer to T. D. and Tal to help out. Annie was the first woman in the state of New Mexico to hold an elected office, having been elected to serve on the Colfax County Commission in 1928. She was very interested in civic affairs and later served as the Democratic County chairwoman on two occasions.

In 1933, Annie received her bid for the position of Eagle Nest Postmaster, a position she held for almost 30 years until she retired from postal service in 1960.

Sonny Johnson, who moved from Red River to Eagle Nest in 1952, held the position between 1960 and 1979 at which time Richard D. Gadry was appointed postmaster. A native of Taunton, Massachusetts, Gadry came to Eagle Nest directly from a position as city delivery carrier in Clovis, New Mexico. Mr. Gadry was postmaster until the current Eagle Nest postmaster, Tese Burt, assumed the position in 1994.

Eagle Nest Government

After working through the preliminaries of incorporation, the first municipal government of Eagle Nest was sworn in July 2, 1976, as the first community in the nation to incorporate during the Bicentennial year.

Frank McCullough, a retired Georgia-Pacific employee and half owner of the lumber yard in Eagle Nest, was sworn in as mayor. Chris Brock,

Scotti Sullivan, Robert Powers and Paul Atzberger were the first elected members of the village council and Gary McBrayer was the first municipal judge. Mayor McCullough died during his first year in office from a heart attack. Chris Brock took up the reins as mayor, followed by Ben Burt who resigned in May 1979 due to possible future conflicts between the mayoral position and his job as Deputy County Sheriff. Burt also cited increased responsibility with the Eagle Nest Baptist Mission as another reason for his resignation. Burt was succeeded by Don Dahl, a member of the village council.

Don Borgeson served as mayor of Eagle Nest on two separate occasions – from 1982 to 1986 and again from 1990 to 1994. Skip Finley was mayor from 1986 to 1988 and Robert Sullivan held the position from 1988 to 1990. Johnny Dahl, was elected for the 1994 to 1998 term.

Eagle Nest School

For many years, students from Elizabethtown, Therma, and Agua Fria attended school at the Moreno Valley School located on the east side of Highway 64 about a mile south of County Road B-8. Students attended elementary through high school in the school house at this location. When this school burned down in 1952, the new school building for grades 1 thru 8 was erected in Eagle Nest in nearly the same location where it sits in 2021. After the original school burned in 1952, high school students were transported to Cimarron High School for classes. The Eagle Nest grade school building has been rebuilt and added to several times since 1952. In 1954, under the School Consolidation Act, the Eagle Nest School became part of the Cimarron School District.

In the 1960s the school had three classrooms—one for the first and second grade; one for the third, fourth, and fifth grades; and one for the sixth, seventh, and eighth grades. An extra room was built on later for the kindergarten. There were approximately seven to eight students per grade.

The social life at school centered around the gymnasium and the cafeteria located just off the gym. Winters were so bad that students spent all their recreation time inside the gym. Basketball was the game of choice. The population was relatively stable at that time and most of the kids who started school together, graduated together.

In the late 1970s, seventh and eighth graders were bused with the high school students to Cimarron for school. In 1993 the seventh grade returned to Eagle Nest, followed by the eighth grade in 1994.

In September 1980, Cimarron School District superintendent Joe Pompeo thought the district was experiencing a "boom" when the Eagle Nest kindergarten class boasted 13 students—five more than they had in 1979. Enrollment at the school that year for grades kindergarten through sixth was 54.

August of 1996 saw 30 kindergarteners enrolled at the first of the year and record numbers in other classes as well, lending to a total enrollment at Eagle Nest Elementary and Middle School of over 250 students. More people with school age children were moving into the Angel Fire/Eagle Nest area.

During the 1960s Joe Torres was principal for the Eagle Nest School followed by Don Dahl. John Romero followed Don Dahl and was the first principal to split his time between Eagle Nest and Cimarron schools. During the 1980 school year Thelma Coker assumed the role of principal, followed by Marla Gadry in 1984 when Coker moved up to accept the position of Cimarron School District superintendent.

Eagle Nest School principal, Lee Mills, started with the school during September 1980 as the third and fourth grade teacher after graduating from the University of New Mexico in 1979 with a specialization in elementary education. He assumed duties as principal in 1991.

Eagle Nest Churches
Currently there are three churches meeting in Eagle Nest.

Members of St. Mel's Catholic Church have been celebrating mass in their own building since 1936, over 85 years. Prior to that time, mass was conducted at the Arko Dancehall located south of Eagle Nest near where County Road B-8 is today.

The Eagle Nest Baptist Church began serving Eagle Nest sometime before 1960 as a mission of the First Baptist Church of Las Vegas. In November 1980, the mission became a full-fledged church while under the care of Pastor Bill Alexander who came to the church in March 1980. Coy Finley was mission pastor until May '79.

Rev. David Denning is the current pastor of Eagle Nest Baptist Church. David and his wife, Donna, arrived in 1994 to lead the congregation.

The Moreno Valley Church of Christ has been a center of worship in the valley for quite a while. Until July 1979 Ernest Arko and his wife, Georganna, led the congregation. When they moved from the area, Darrell Powell and Duane Smith of Dumas, Texas assumed the duties as ministers.

The congregation, meeting two and a half miles south of Eagle Nest, is currently led by Delbert McLoud.

Eagle Nest Lake

Eagle Nest Lake has been a favorite fishing spot since the dam was completed in 1918, bringing a flood of tourists to this small mountain community. As it is today, tourism has always been one of the primary economic forces in the success of Eagle Nest.

During 1977 and 1978 Eagle Nest Lake was closed to public fishing due to low water levels. The lake diminished to 6,000 acre-feet, one of the lowest recorded levels since the completion of the dam. The closure caused a severe economic impact on the village when the traditional fishing-oriented tourism population lost their main reason to come to Eagle Nest.

Then, in 1979, near-record spring run-off brought the level of the lake back up to 48,000 acre-feet, half of the lake's 100,000 designed capacity. The New Mexico Department of Game and Fish entered into a temporary lease agreement with CS Ranch during June 1979 to again open the lake to the public. The success of the season was good enough to warrant extending the lease five more months to April 30, 1980, allowing winter fishing on the lake.

Due to the persuasion of State Senators John Morrow and C.B. Trujillo, the 1980 state legislature designated $320,000 from the state general fund to acquire a ten-year lease on Eagle Nest Lake. The lease, signed by Department of Game and Fish Director Harold Olson and State Game Commission Chairman Edward Munoz representing the state, and J. Leslie Davis and Linda M. Davis representing CS Ranch, was effective May 1, 1980 through April 30, 1990.

A formal ceremony was held May 24, 1980 to honor Senators Morrow and Trujillo for their part in convincing the legislature to fund the lease of

Eagle Nest Lake. Former state senator and area resident Bill Gallagher presided over the ceremonies which included speeches by Governor Bruce King, Representative Kelly Mora, and Game and Fish Director Harold Olson.

During June 1980, the Game and Fish Department netted and gave away several tons of suckers and chubs in order reduce their populations (estimated at 400,000 pounds), which competed with the trout the anglers preferred to catch.

The lease with the state was renewed in 1990 to run until the year 2000, and then extended again until 2002. In 2002 the Davis Family sold Eagle Nest Lake to the State of New Mexico, so now the land around the Lake is managed by New Mexico State Parks. The water in the lake is managed by the Interstate Stream Commission, and New Mexico Game & Fish manage fishing in the Lake.

Spirits of Eagle Nest

Eagle Nest was not always just a quiet little farming community. It was a rough and rowdy ranch town that catered to the entertainment of cowboys and tourists. While at times it could be peaceful and calm, at other times it could be as turbulent as the waters of Eagle Nest Lake during high winds.

Some in the area believe it was this rough and rowdy side of Eagle Nest that led to certain "ghosts" remaining behind. Whether or not you have leanings to believe in a spirit world, the ghost stories of Eagle Nest add a colorful flavor.

On certain nights at the Laguna Vista, it is said a woman in period dance-hall dress visits some of the customers before disappearing toward the site of the hidden staircase.

In the kitchen at Julio's, pots and pans are thrown about the room and items move from where they have been put away to some place totally impractical.

Next door to Julio's lives the spirit of a woman who dislikes men. She plays endless pranks on the men who cross the threshold of what was once her door—at least those who come and act as though they plan to stay for a while.

Eagle Nest Today

Although it has its share of ghost stories, Eagle Nest is far from a ghost town. According to the 1990 census the village had a population of 189. In the 2010 census, that number had grown to 290 residents.

Relatively quiet during the winter, the spring, summer, and fall months bring a bumper crop of fishermen to the area. R.V. parks are full. Lodges, restaurants, and shops are inundated with tourists. It is estimated that 1.5 million people pass through Eagle Nest each year.

On July 4th the village offers one of the best fireworks displays in the state, releasing blossoming missiles so that the colorful explosions are reflected in the waters of Eagle Nest Lake.

The last weekend of July has been set aside in recent years for the High Country Arts Fest. The juried show pulls in artists from all over New Mexico as well as from many neighboring states. In 1996 Arts Fest participants were entertained by the musical group Ancient Winds playing music from the Andes Mountains.

Another recent event, Fish Fest, has drawn extra attention to Eagle Nest Lake during September. Tagged fish, worth high prize money, are released into the lake to be caught by lucky fishermen. The lake normally has a large number of boats moving around, but during Fish Fest boats appear almost hull-to-hull while people stand side-by-side on the shore.

Perhaps Eagle Nest has been transformed from the quiet stream where native tribes collected feathers to a bustling community, but it still exemplifies the free-soaring spirit of the eagles that continue to rise above the community on the shores of Eagle Nest Lake.

* * *

Jo Bynum graduated from Howard Payne University in 1977 with a BGS degree (which basically means she couldn't decide what she wanted to do with her life). After over 20 years of office clerical experience, Jo is finally pursuing the career she has always wanted—writing. She worked as editor for the Sangre de Cristo Chronicle while spending time at home on her fiction creations. Jo lived in Black Lake with her husband, Ronnie and two children, Jon Paul and Holly, before relocating to Texas.

The Vietnam Veterans National Memorial

by Mike McDonald, Vietnam Veteran
Ninth Infantry Div., 1967-1968

It was May 22, 1968, and I was in Vietnam. My assignment was with the Headquarters, Headquarters Company of the Ninth Infantry Division at Bear Cat, a base carved out of the jungle, and located about five miles from Bien Hoa, home of the U.S. Army Headquarters of Vietnam. I had the privilege of being in the Ninth Infantry Division Band, so regardless of almost nightly shelling by rockets and mortars from the Viet Cong, it was a fairly safe assignment in a country actively engaged in war. I was glad I was not involved in combat. However, on that same date, in another part of Vietnam, a deadly fire fight would occur that would change the lives of many people and alter the landscape of Moreno Valley.

At 5:20 p.m. on that day, I was preparing to go to the mess hall for dinner. At precisely that moment in the Quang Tri Province near Con Thien, B Company of the 1st Battalion, 4th Marines, was ambushed by a large force of Vietnamese Army regulars.

They had left Yankee Station on the 20th of May in a patrol sweep of Con Thien. Two days went by with no enemy encounters and the 22nd arrived, hot and humid but clear, and the troops, although prepared, were expecting another long, hot but uneventful walk through the bush. The waist high Kunie grass brushed their elbows as they maneuvered around thick brush and hedgerows.

Out on point was B company, led by Lt. David Westphall. As the soldiers approached a long, low rise, a sudden volley of machine gun, grenade and mortar fire flew into their midst. The CO, Captain Robert Harris, immediately ordered return fire, but no enemy could be seen. Then, almost as suddenly as the firing had started, approximately 100 soldiers of the Vietnamese Army came charging toward B Company, firing their weapons into the forward positions. Captain Harris ran up to take over a machine gun from a wounded gunner and was shot through the heart. Lt. Westphall, along with his radioman, Charles Kirkland, was attempting to move a squad up to the firing line when both were strafed with machine guns and fell dead. The battle raged ferociously for twenty minutes before the 2nd Platoon could relieve the situation and drive back the enemy. Thirteen Marines died and 27 were wounded.

Captain Harris could have been on his way to his next assignment but wanted to stay on long enough to be sure the new CO had a good orientation and would treat his men right. Lt. Westphall had been due for R&R (rest and relaxation) but had not pressed the matter. Radioman Kirkland stayed loyally by his lieutenant's side. These men put their devotion to duty and loyalty before personal considerations, and it cost them their lives.

Five days later, in the peaceful Moreno Valley of Northern New Mexico, Dr. Victor Westphall was working on his ranch, Val Verde, when a car arrived, and two marine captains got out and approached him.

"Are you Dr. Westphall?" they asked.

Victor replied in the affirmative.

"Your son has been killed," they said.

In his book, *David's Story, A Casualty of Vietnam*, Dr. Westphall recalls that moment. "I heard, but for long moments I could not, would not, comprehend. The newcomers before me, the awful moment of their visitation now complete, were all compassion and twice offered to help me down. As my feet touched earth a single piteous word hesitantly and tenderly escaped me, expressing a question that conveyed faint hope as well as a request for confirmation and identity.

"David?"

"Victor," they answered.

The glimmer of hope was gone. Our son's name was Victor David.

The news devastated David's mother, Jeanne, and it took her some time to recover, but in the end, it was she who inspired her husband.

David was buried in the National Cemetery in Santa Fe, New Mexico, and after the funeral, Victor and Jeanne discussed the possibility of using David's $30,000 insurance policy as the basis for a scholarship fund in his name, but that was soon discarded as too banal. They wanted to do something extraordinary to reflect David's life and to honor all those who fought in Vietnam. Jeanne came up with the idea for a non-denominational chapel that should be called the Vietnam Veterans Peace and Brotherhood Chapel, and Victor loved it. But where could it be located?

For years Victor had been successful in the building business in Albuquerque, but three years earlier he had decided to pursue his other interest … writing history. While in pursuit of this goal he bought Val Verde Ranch in the Moreno Valley, and it was at this residence that David spent the last time with his parents just prior to being shipped to Vietnam.

On that visit, David hiked in a straight line from the ranch to a point midway up Wheeler Peak, the highest point in New Mexico, just to prove his readiness as a Marine. He liked to sit on a particular promontory overlooking the valley while he read or pondered. David was not only athletic—a football player and track star in high school and college—but he was also quite intelligent, very literate, and wrote essays and poetry. One of David's favorite stories as a child, and one that he continued to love as an adult, was a book called *Wings For Per*. The last passage in that book reads:

The Vietnam Veterans National Memorial in Angel Fire, NM
(photo by Elaine Jarzen)

"Then I will fly up into the clear, washed air of spring and soar over the eagle's nest and over my home under the crag. Mother will stand in front of the house and clasp her hands in wonder. She will say: 'Look, Per has wings'."

Victor looked to that promontory that overlooked the valley, also known as Eagle's Nest, and envisioned it as the perfect spot for the chapel. Soon after the funeral, Victor contacted Ted Luna, a Santa Fe architect, to design the chapel, with these words to guide him: "The structure should be such that no person entering it could leave with quite the same attitude toward peace and war." The preliminary drawings were done by July 7th, 1968, and Victor considered them to be magnificent and inspired, and he began construction almost immediately.

There were many attempts to obtain grants and other financing, but to no avail, as the social and political atmosphere at the time was not favorable for such an undertaking. But Victor plodded on and did most of the construction himself with his own money.

However, there came a time when he needed to raise some heavy beams to the ceiling; he became quite despondent thinking that it was just beyond his means and that he could never finish such a project alone. At that moment, a young itinerant carpenter, who happened to have all his tools with him, came onto the property asking if there was any work he could do. Victor and the young carpenter finished the ceiling, and then the carpenter went his way. The help that was needed came. Victor cites that as an inspiring period during the construction of the chapel, and it gave him added hope that the chapel was meant to be built.

Soon after the initial construction, Victor began locking the door of the chapel. One morning when he arrived to continue his work, he found a message scrawled on a piece of scrap plywood: "Why did you lock me out when I needed to come in?" The chapel has never been locked since then.

As the work progressed, it started to gain some attention. On May 22, 1971, three years to the day after David's death, Victor felt the construction was far enough along to have a dedication ceremony. It drew the three national television networks as well as A.P., U.P.I. and N.E.A. wire services. In the summer of 1972, Gloria Emerson of the *New York Times* visited the chapel and was inspired to write an article about it, telling Victor, "Thank you for teaching me how to cry. I thought that I had forgotten how."

As the years went by, many people would stop to see the beautiful soaring building that dominated the promontory, and word slowly filtered out into the world that here was something to which attention should be paid. Attitudes changed slowly, and the idea of such a memorial became more acceptable. But there was still some controversy over the chapel's purpose.

On November 4, 1979, an article appeared in *Parade* magazine by Michael Satchell about the chapel. It cited Victor's point that the chapel was for all Vietnam Veterans ... of *both* sides. In fact, Victor's actual dedication is: "For all Vietnam veterans: the living, the dead, and the maimed in body and spirit." He made no distinction as to nationality. In his own words from the book, *David's Story, A Casualty of Vietnam*, Victor replied to the controversy.

"It is the nature of human language that it is impossible to encompass absolute meaning of a complex subject in a single phrase, sentence, or perhaps even paragraph. Sometimes it is difficult to embrace full understanding in even an extended presentation. This truism of human nature is difficult to understand for persons who see everything as either all black or all white.

"First, and foremost, the Vietnam Veterans Peace and Brotherhood Chapel is, as its name implies, a monument to peace—not a war memorial. On this point I am adamant. If full implementation of the concept of peace demands the Christian attitude of extending the hand of fellowship to former enemies, I will not demure. This whole matter of friends and enemies is, after all, an ephemeral thing. Given the complexities of international relations as they are practiced by the human race, today's enemies may well be tomorrow's friends."

The controversy over the fact that the chapel was for *all* Vietnam veterans was short-lived, however, and advocates for its increased importance began to make things happen. By 1975 bills had been introduced in the House and Senate to make the chapel a national monument, but a dozen more years would go by before that happened. Other things *were* happening, however.

In 1977, Dick Wilson of the Disabled American Veterans contacted Victor regarding possible financial support from that organization. On August 5, 1977, the first annual check of $10,000 arrived. In October of 1981, the DAV became even more involved and formed the DAV Vietnam Veterans National Memorial, Inc. which turned into a $2,000,000 venture that would eventually include a visitors' center. Construction on that broke ground on May 28th, 1984, with appropriate remarks by Senator Pete Domenici. The building was opened on a limited basis to the public on August 10, 1985, and even then, designer Mark Barensfeld was planning the interior detailing. The center's interior is so stunningly original that it vies with the chapel for inspiration.

On May 26, 1986, thousands of visitors arrived at the memorial for the visitors' center's official dedication. It was a day of reflection and camaraderie as most of those attending were Vietnam veterans. The ribbon cutting ceremony at the visitors' center along with appropriate remarks by inspiring speakers made the day memorable. In 1987, the United States Congress gave the memorial its national recognition, and on November 16, President Ronald Reagan signed a proclamation to that effect. In part the document reads:

"The Congress, by Public Law 100-164, approved November 13, 1987, has recognized the Disabled American Veterans Vietnam Veterans National Memorial as a memorial of national significance and requested the President to issue a proclamation in observance thereof."

The proclamation also contained these words:

"NOW, THEREFORE, I, RONALD REAGAN, President of the United States of America ... also salute the efforts of the individuals who have made possible the creation and continued existence of this memorial."

The chapel and visitors' center are now called The Vietnam Veterans National Memorial. It took almost twenty years before this parents' vision of a memorial to their son, and the men and women with whom he served, gained the national respect it so well deserves.

It was the first Vietnam memorial, before The Wall in Washington and before all others. Its white wings soar above the floor of the Moreno Valley, beckoning all to come and honor those who served their country in one of the most controversial conflicts our nation has witnessed. Once you enter into its serenity, all that is forgotten, and the only memory becomes that of the people who participated, including some 58,000 who gave their lives in that conflict. Among them was 28-year-old 1st Lieutenant Victor David Westphall III, U.S.M.C.

These two inscriptions, taken from a poem and an essay by David Westphall, appear on the walls of the chapel:

Greed plowed cities desolate
Lust ran snorting thru the streets
Pride reared up to desecrate
Shrines, and there were no retreats.
So man learned to shed the tears
With which he measures out his years.

At the sight of the heavenly
throne Ezekiel fell on his
face, but the voice of God
commanded, "Son of man, stand
upon your feet and I will
speak with you." If we are to
stand on our feet in the
presence of God, what, then,
is one man that he should
debase the dignity of another?

The story of the genesis of the Vietnam Veterans National Memorial is fascinating, but the everyday inspiration it provides is what makes it more than just a beautiful structure. An example of that was told to me by Linda Vaughn, the memorial's administrative assistant.

On his numerous travels across the country, Linda's father loved to drive through the Moreno Valley, and watch the progress being made on the chapel. He was a florist and loved to watch things grow to fruition. Little did Linda know at the time, that years later she would be working here. She and her father both agreed that God had called her to this place.

Vietnam veterans come to the memorial on an almost daily basis and

Linda has talked to many of them, but one such veteran will always stand out in her mind. He had had an extremely hard time adjusting to civilian life after his return from the war when he began feeling that he just could not handle it anymore and had decided to take his life. A friend of his had once been a volunteer at the chapel and told him of it. He wanted to visit it as a final act.

One day as Linda was sitting at her desk, the man came to her and asked if his friend still worked there. She replied that he did not and asked him if she could help. He answered that she could not and went back out into the Veterans Room. He was sitting on one of the benches when a voice inside her told Linda to go out to him. She was upset. She was very busy and needed to get some work done, but the voice persisted until finally she went to him, put her hand on his shoulder and asked, "Can I help?"

For two uninterrupted hours, Linda listened as he poured out his story to her. There was no judgment and no advice given, just the opportunity for him to relate his history the way he wanted it to be remembered. A little later, the man's girlfriend called the local law enforcement agency warning that he had a shotgun. She feared he might do harm to himself or others.

Linda received a phone call from them asking if she had seen him and if she knew where he was. She did, but refused to give them the information, fearing a confrontation with the law would put him over the edge. Instead, she went to him herself, and found him to be fine and willing to face his life again. The visit to the memorial had saved his life, and he often returns to this place that now means so much to him. He calls it Heaven and he calls Linda his guardian angel.

The memorial is not a static structure. It is a breathing entity built with blood and tears. It holds the memory of thousands of lives sacrificed in their youth for what they felt was the honor of their country. By coincidence, the soaring west wall of the chapel points in a direct line to Wheeler Peak, the tallest mountain in New Mexico, as if beckoning us to look to a higher source of inspiration other than itself. Visiting the memorial can be a very moving experience.

I watched as Victor Westphall built the chapel and have visited several times since. I am fine as I show friends and relatives all the different aspects of the chapel. They divert me. However, when I enter the chapel alone, I cannot help being extremely moved and touched emotionally as I ponder what it stands for and why it was built. It wasn't a government or private commission that brought about the chapel. It was only, and simply … love … that raised the walls.

* * *

Michael "Mike" McDonald is a Vietnam veteran, having served from September 1967 to September 1968 with the 9th Infantry. He resided in Santa Fe for twenty years and became acquainted with Dr. Victor Westphall in the early '70s when his family vacationed in the Idlewild community. Mike has, for many years, been interested in New Mexico history. He is the author of "The Quiz of Enchantment" published by New Mexico Magazine in 1992. He now lives in New York with his wife, Barbara, who helps proofread and edit his writing.

Dr. Victor Westphall

Founder of Vietnam Veterans National Memorial
Angel Fire, New Mexico

By Elaine V. Sandberg-Jarzen

High on a hill overlooking the tranquil Moreno Valley, a sacred monument rises gently from the earth. Its curving, outstretched wings beckon war torn veterans and families who have lost loved ones to enter. Once inside, these fragile survivors are embraced in loving arms and are comforted by two simple words "Welcome Home." The healing process has begun ...

When Dr. Victor Westphall purchased the Val Verde Ranch in 1966, he never dreamed that he would build the nation's first memorial to Vietnam Veterans. "There was no reason for me to make the move from Albuquerque to Northern New Mexico except that I felt a compulsion to do so," explains Victor.

Two years later, on May 22, 1968, his oldest son David was killed in action in Con Thien, South Vietnam. Victor then knew the reason why he moved—to build an enduring symbol of the tragedy and futility of the war. Using David's insurance money, Dr. Westphall started construction of the chapel. He writes, "We (his family) hoped that a memorial would serve as a national symbol of the sacrifices of Vietnam Veterans and a source of inspiration for the pursuit of a peaceful world."

Dr. Westphall's vision of erecting a memorial began to materialize after he hired a young architect named Ted Luna from Santa Fe. Luna designed a gull-like structure, rising 50 feet above the ground. When asked what role he played in building the chapel, Victor replied, "I did some of all of it and all of a lot of it." The initial construction was assigned to contractor George Vedler. Before the walls were finished, Vedler left for Norway to visit his mother. That winter, a storm destroyed a portion of

114

the main wall which had to be re-done the following spring.

Drawing upon his previous building experience, Victor designed a 20-foot template so that the chapel walls would lay to a true curve. He recalls an inspirational event that occurred during construction.

"While sitting on the scaffolding I had built," he says, "I wondered how in heaven's name I was going to put together an intricate ceiling structure by myself. My prayers were answered a short time later when a young carpenter walked in the door. After talking to him awhile, I found out he happened to have his tools with him and hired him on the spot."

The monument was completed three years after David's death and was dedicated on May 22, 1971. Victor decided that there would be 13 photos placed inside the chapel. David's photo remains in the memorial year round, while the other 12 are rotated on a monthly basis. Dr. Westphall also installed a 13-foot-high cross in the chapel and flew the initial 13 star flag of our nation. A year and a half later, he was surprised to learn that there were 13 killed in the company in which his son lost his life.

Jeanne Westphall, Victor's wife, initially named the memorial The Vietnam Veterans Peace and Brotherhood Chapel. In 1977, the Disabled American Veterans (DAV) pledged their support to Victor, assuming ownership of the building with the understanding that they would perpetuate it for all time. The chapel's name was changed in 1983 to "The DAV Vietnam Veterans National Memorial."

Construction of a Visitor's Center began in 1984 and was completed a year later by contractor Mike Laverty. It is largely underground so as not to detract from the memorial chapel which is the focal point of the entire complex.

The interior, designed by Mark Barensfeld, consists of color photographs taken in Vietnam, along with hanging emblems of various military units. Panels located throughout the 6,000 square foot Visitor's Center contain statistics regarding the war. From 1962 through 1985, there were over 58,000 Americans killed in Vietnam. Another 303,704 were wounded. The average age of an American soldier was 19.

Of the estimated 11,500 women who had tours of duty in Vietnam, eight died in the war, all of them nurses. A miniature bronze statue of the Women's Vietnam Veterans National Memorial located in Washington

D.C. is exhibited. The sculpture, created by artist Glenna Goodacre from Santa Fe, depicts three women. One woman tends to an injured soldier, while the second one holds the soldier's helmet. A third woman is standing, searching skyward. Diane Carlson Evans, founder of the women's project, said the statue is for all women: military, civilians, volunteers, and relief workers who served in the Southeast Asian country.

The Visitor's Center also has a state-of-the-art, Kiosk Learning Environment Computer System. It contains information from casualty reports provided by the Department of Defense on all veterans who died in the Vietnam War. With just the touch of a finger, visitors can locate information on over 58,000 deceased veterans by their name, rank, branch, date of birth, casualty date, hometown, and state. For example, the database can compute the total number of casualties from each state in just a matter of seconds. It can also calculate the number of deaths in each branch of service—Army, Navy, Air Force, Marine Corps, and Coast Guard.

The public can receive a history lesson on the Vietnam War via the Kiosk Learning System by accessing a program entitled, "America & Vietnam—The War Years." This module contains actual footage taken in Vietnam of Search and Rescue, Tunnel Rats, River Patrol Boats, Door Gunners, etc. A geography section is also available where users can view maps of Vietnam and battle locations. An Almanac Module, containing a day-by-day chronology of the events that occurred during the Vietnam War, was later added to the database.

The Memorial often receives inquiries from the staff of the Vietnam National Memorial (The Wall) in Washington D.C. Individuals having difficulty searching for and locating names of deceased Vietnam Veterans are referred to the Memorial in Angel Fire where the Kiosk Computer System comes to the rescue. Tourists can also view an ongoing video titled "Dear America, Letters Home From Vietnam."

The center currently exhibits more than 1,300 donated photos of deceased veterans, along with accompanying biographies. In addition, visitors can page through a directory containing the names of all deceased veterans that are inscribed on the "Wall" in Washington D.C. Veterans who are searching for surviving buddies from Vietnam can look through the Memorial's "Keep in Touch" books, sorted by type of military service, then the name of the individual.

Memorial Day activities at the Vietnam Veterans National Memorial attract thousands of visitors to Angel Fire from all over the United States. Prior to the ceremonies, a group of veterans and their families carry a 30x50 foot American flag high above their heads. Participants march in cadence from the blinking light, where Hwy. 434 intersects Hwy. 64, about a quarter of a mile up to the Memorial. Keynote speakers over the years have included Dennis Joyner, President of the Vietnam Veterans National Memorial; the Honorable Jesse Brown, Secretary of Veteran Affairs; General William Westmoreland; Bill Coors, CEO, Adolph Coors Company, and Bill Demby, Outstanding Disabled Veteran of the Year, just to name a few. Helicopters from the NM Army National Guard fly overhead, followed by jets from the NM Air National Guard. Talented musicians perform highly emotional and inspirational songs throughout the ceremony. Mary Teater, past National Commander of Gold Star Mothers of America, annually presents a wreath.

On the eve of Memorial Day, a POW/MIA Candlelight Vigil is held inside the chapel. The names of over 2,500 Prisoners of War and Vietnam Veterans Missing In Action were read by volunteers during the 1994 ceremony.

Dr. Westphall celebrated the 25th anniversary of the dedication of the Memorial Chapel on May 22, 1996. When asked how many people have gone through the chapel, Victor replied, "At the present time, we have from 65 to 75 thousand visitors a year, so you can determine how many we have had in the past quarter of a century."

Dr. Westphall describes two interesting stories about Vietnam veterans. "A lot of people have difficulty at first in coming here," says Victor. "They don't know what they are going to experience." He recalls an instance when an attorney from Taos left a plant for David by the rear door but didn't enter the building until the following year. He also tells of a veteran who lived back east and drove as far as Taos. He then turned around and went back home without coming to the chapel. A few years later, the same vet drove to the entrance of the monument and had every inclination to leave, but decided, "This is ridiculous!"

Victor says, "It took a supreme act of will for him to come that quarter of a mile from Highway 64 to the memorial. Many people who find enough courage to enter the building are universally glad that they did because they find peace and solace here."

For several years, Dr. Westphall had entertained the idea of going to Vietnam to visit the ambush site where David was killed. "I really don't know exactly why, but there was some compulsion urging me on to do that," explained Victor.

In the spring of 1994, Victor, his younger son Douglas, Jim Goss, an RN from Pennsylvania, and Gerry Schooler, the tour director, left for Vietnam. They flew from Los Angeles to Taipei and then in a smaller plane to Saigon. The next morning, they flew to Da Nang. From there they drove to Con Thien located on the DMZ. Dr. Westphall recalls, "The first day we were there, we walked up to the top of 500-foot tall Con Thien hill which was the highest point in that entire region. It was fought over and sought by the North Vietnamese, South Vietnamese, and the Americans."

Their guide, Mr. Chin, turned out to be the interpreter for the same Marine Corps battalion that David belonged to. With his aid, the battalion journal for May 22, 1968, and an artillery grid map of the area, the group was able to locate exactly where the ambush took place. A rubber tree plantation covers the battleground today.

Victor found remarkable coincidences while in Vietnam. The road around Con Thien is almost identical in shape with the east wall of the chapel. In addition, the name Con Thien is Vietnamese for 'Place of Angels.' Victor scattered a sample of earth taken from the DAV Memorial site and brought back soil from Con Thien to be scattered at the memorial in Angel Fire. He found that the soil from both locations was almost identical—a reddish, fine textured clay. The similarities between the two locations half a world apart provided Victor with the answer to the burning question as to "why" he was compelled to go to Vietnam!

On September 14, 1998, the DAV returned ownership of the Memorial back to Dr. Westphall. The property was then transferred to the David Westphall Veterans Foundation (DWVF). "We need to raise substantial sums of money to perpetuate the memorial," explains Victor, "and we are confident that the public will come generously to our aid."

The New Mexico Army National Guard donated a UH-1H "Huey"

helicopter to the Vietnam Veterans Memorial. It was placed on a concrete cradle designed by Ted Luna of Santa Fe, the original architect of the chapel. Dedication of the Huey took place on Sunday, May 30, 1999. Lawrence McDonald, who piloted the helicopter in Vietnam, spoke to the crowd during the ceremony. On Easter Sunday in 1967, the Vietcong attacked a battalion of Republic troops near Vinh Long, west of Saigon. McDonald agreed to fly the Huey known as "Viking Surprise" into battle, laying down a smoke screen so other helicopters could rescue the troops. During the mission, the aircraft was bombarded with 133 enemy rounds and the pilot was hit with shrapnel. McDonald received a Purple Heart and Silver Star and was recognized for saving the lives of at least 20 Americans and South Vietnamese.

The Memorial staff worked with TRACOM to obtain a Bell AH-1 Cobra Helicopter, and hoped to have it delivered by Veterans Day 1999. The Cobra is the first true armed helicopter containing gunships and was used in Vietnam to fly protective cover for the smaller "Huey."

Visitors express their heartfelt gratitude to Dr. Westphall when touring the Vietnam Veterans National Memorial in Angel Fire, New Mexico. This historical monument not only pays tribute to the American heroes of Vietnam but to the men and women veterans of *all* wars. The Memorial will stand as an enduring symbol, reminding future generations to **not forget those who sacrificed their lives in the name of freedom ...**

On July 22, 2003, Dr. Victor Westphall passed at the Memorial. His wife Jeanne Westphall passed a year later on August 1, 2004. They are buried on the grounds of the Memorial.

In 2004 the David Westphall Veterans Foundation approached the state of New Mexico, seeking another source of funding. On Veterans Day 2005 the site became the Vietnam Veterans Memorial State Park.

While under NM State Parks, the State completed several renovations and improvements. The amphitheater was the first of these. The Phase I project also included a new roof, stucco and furnace for the chapel. Phase II improvements for renovation of the Visitor's Center were completed in 2010.

On July 1, 2017, management of the Memorial was transferred

from the NM State Parks to NM Department of Veterans Services and is home to the Chapel, the Visitor's Center/Vietnam War Museum, the Huey helicopter which saw action in Vietnam during the war, the Veterans Memorial Walkway, a Gift Shop, Memorial Gardens, an amphitheater, as well as the gravesites of Jeanne and Victor Westphall. The Memorial still welcomes over 45,000 visitors annually.

In 2018, the State of New Mexico announced that a new veterans cemetery would be opened adjacent to the Memorial, and the first interment took place there in July, 2021.

Volunteers play an important role in the daily operation of the Visitor's Center. If you are interested in obtaining more information about the Vietnam Veterans National Memorial, please write to: P.O. Box 608, Angel Fire, NM 87710. Call (575) 377 6900, or visit their website at vietnamveteransmemorial.org

* * *

Elaine Sandberg-Jarzen is a freelance photographer and writer. She received her B.S. Degree in Business and M.A. Degree in Education from the University of Northern Colorado in Greeley. Elaine and her husband, Phil, moved to Angel Fire in 1992 from Denver, Colorado. She was a member of the Moreno Valley Writers Guild, Angel Fire Historical Society and the Santa Fe Trail Association. For two years, she was a disc jockey playing "oldies" on KAFR radio in Angel Fire.

Fire Of The Gods And Angels

(Angel Fire)

By Martin H. Andrews

"There is an angel in the mountain. She is lying down. Her head, wings, torso, and waist seem to form where the 'quad lift' starts; then her legs and feet are down toward the south. She can best be seen when one is coming down from Palo Flechado Pass, where the highway turns straight, and from a few places along Highway 434, when there is snow in the valley." —— Sally LeBus

Fire of the Gods and Angels

Looking through ageless eyes, one could witness the complete, chaotic, geologic history of Moreno Valley; this remarkably beautiful, pristine hanging valley ... the result of vast cataclysmic volcanic activity, unimaginable compressive forces squeezing land north and south, simultaneously folding and thrusting complex mountain ridges, later to be washed over and submerged by seas in the lower areas. Stark beauty remained after the waters gradually found access to sloping regions eastward and southward, establishing, eventually, the fertile green valley.

Eons and countless centuries later, and more than two centuries before the arrival of any Anglos in these mountains, the Moache Ute Indians, a fierce, nomadic, constantly warring tribe migrating to this region, probably from what is now Utah, found a special gathering place far up on the mountainside rising from the eastern side of the valley and toward the southern end of the valley. They claimed this area for their Indian summer and fall camps, and forever since, that sacred area has been called the Valley of the Utes.

One legend describes such an autumnal renewal of the tribe's ancestral ties with the Great Spirit: Early on the first morning of the ceremonials, three young braves who had been out on a hunting trip came back to the camp with news of a strange, fiery glow at the tip of the mountain. The Utes were uneasy as they gazed at the mysterious tongues of red and orange licking at the morning sky.

One of the elders broke the silence:

"It is an omen ... the fire of the gods and the angels ... blessing our celebration."

In awe of the miracle, the Utes accepted this explanation.

While they were encamped there, all of the Utes occasionally witnessed those dazzling fire-like displays atop the mountain when the sun crested over the rim of the peak, beaming through frost-encrusted trees. Equally spectacular in the evenings, were the waning multi-hued sunset rays meeting the fluffy white clouds making their ascent behind the mountain. The almost celestial color and light must have caused the Utes to spiritualize the visual experience and to name the mountain, in their language, "Fire of the gods and angels."

Franciscan friars, following the trails of the Indian mountain men, came into the Sangre de Cristo Mountains searching for new souls to convert. Many of the mountains had taken on Spanish names, and the peak above the Ute's hallowed ground was called Agua Fria. As the friars mingled with the Utes and learned of the omen and miracle they described, and indeed witnessed it themselves, they concurred with the Ute's vivid name for the mountain, except to delete 'gods,' being that they were Christian and followers of the one and only God. As a result of the influence of the friars, Agua Fria became known as "the place of the fire of the angels." Now bearing the imprint of both Indian and Spanish cultures, the legend persisted and was strengthened by trappers who traveled to Taos with tales of strange lights glowing above Agua Fria.

The formation of the Maxwell Land Grant (originally the Beaubien-Miranda Land Grant) in 1841 assured a continuation of the legend, because it was shortly thereafter that the famous guide and mountaineer, Christopher "Kit" Carson, who was an agent for the Utes, and was then living in Cimarron, told his friend, Lucien B. Maxwell, that he, too, had observed this unusual light effect at dawn and dusk, especially during the fall and early winter months, accrediting it to brilliant sunlight striking the hoar frost on tree branches.

Carson, with a knowledge of Spanish, English, and the Ute languages, according to best legend in the year 1845, translated the Ute's descriptive phrase into "Angel Fire," a name which replaced Agua Fria for the mountain. More than a century later it was chosen by the LeBus family as the name for the ski, golf, and fishing resort the family envisioned and began to build on and near the mountain.

It was in 1954 that Roy and George F. LeBus, who had been successful in oil and ranching in the Wichita Falls, Texas area, purchased the Monte Verde Ranch (just under 9,000 acres) from the Orville Bullingtons for ten dollars an acre. The Bullington and the LeBus families had been friends in Wichita Falls. The LeBus family not only continued and increased the cattle ranching business, but also developed a wood treatment (pole) industry at the small community known as Agua Fria, near the corner of Highway 64 and old State Road 38 (now Highway 434).

They subsequently purchased another 14,000 acres, comprising the old Cieneguilla Ranch, at twelve dollars per acre, from the Maxwell Land Grant, thus amassing for the family all of the valley area now comprising the Angel Fire Resort and township. (Bullington had originally obtained the Monte Verde ranchland from the Maxwell Land Grant.) The southernmost boundary of the Cieneguilla Ranch was also the southwestern border of the original Maxwell Land Grant, now identical with the southernmost border of present-day Angel Fire. A rock-pile (cairn) marking that point, still exists, about a mile west of the Monte Verde Lake. Thus, with the acquisition of Cieneguilla in 1956, the Monte Verde Corporation was born.

A decade later, the LeBus families sat and reminisced following a Sunday dinner in the old "Rock House." (This house had already been built on the Monte Verde ranch by the Bullingtons and is located just to the east of Hwy. 64, between Agua Fria and Eagle Nest. In the late 1990s it was operated as a bed and breakfast enterprise by Sally LeBus, Roy's daughter).

Other than trips back to Texas, and to Colorado, Red River or Taos to ski in winter, the LeBus family's days, months and years were occupied by their business interests in the Valley. They all enjoyed skiing, and on that particular Sunday afternoon in the 1960s, the discussion focus was on the perceptible decline of the cattle ranching business generally, and on the burgeoning of snow-skiing and winter sports. Roy, especially, had begun to consider alternative uses of the land.

George (son of Roy and nephew of George F.) was more to the point. "We ought to put in a little runt tow down here, where we won't have to go to Red River or Taos skiin' all the time."

Roy, his dad, then said, "Well, I've been thinking about that!"

It is George's present day recollection that … "Well, he was thinkin' a little bigger than I was thinkin'!"

Turned out that Roy already believed a good ski area could be planned and built on Agua Fria (Angel Fire) mountain. And, as the Sunday afternoon conversation became more animated and enthusiastic, they envisioned the development, not just of a ski area, but also of a golf course and a lake, with accompanying amenities, along with the platting of building sites and roads for future growth and development. The building of an air strip was also planned. Even a new name for the nascent resort was discussed, since none of them thought the name "Monte Verde" to be the best, especially for the ski resort.

It was, once again, George who suggested, "Let's call it *Angel Fire!*"

And they all, then and there, agreed!

Almost immediately, and throughout 1966-67, building plans and construction proceeded at a feverish pace. Across four miles of road from Highway 64, and onto a dirt landing strip, workers and supplies were brought in, and within a year and a half, the early ski trails were cut, the Monte Verde Lake was constructed, and a nine-hole golf course designed and built.

John and Kathryn Cardwell, the first to build a home in the area (located adjacent to what became the "practice putting green") figured prominently in those early days. They were employed by the corporation, he as head of construction and maintenance; she as secretary. John cut trees for the ski trails, pushing them aside into the surrounding trees. He also cut trees for some of the early roads leading into the base area, and the sections which had been subdivided for future building lots and recreation areas. Eight sections were first subdivided: Monte Verde Units I, II, and III; Angel Fire Units I, II, and IV; Monte Verde Lake, Monte Verde V, Unit I. A large metal building from the pole treatment plant at Agua Fria was moved to the ski trail for a base lodge, and later served as the core building for the enlarged base lodge.

Skiing rapidly became a popular winter sport and as word spread about the new Angel Fire Resort via television, radio, magazines, and newspapers, and by word of mouth, people were drawn to the area from Texas, Oklahoma, Kansas, and New Mexico, creating a need for lodging accommodations. The first ones constructed were modular stacked units, called Fireside Lodge, later renamed North Wind. They were completed in 1971. The following year, the Villa Condominiums were built, later taking on the name The French Henry (after Henry Buruel, the Frenchman who mined gold on Baldy Mountain). Soon thereafter, the construction of a club house and a large lodge was begun.

Meanwhile, continuous outflow of cash to finance the rapid development, along with limited return on their investment, and the inevitable spiral of expenses associated with a more lavish lifestyle, the LeBus families became interested in divesting themselves of most of the land and the resort facilities. They had, in fact, already sold their cattle in 1966, and in 1969 an investment group, with Glen Miller from Wisconsin, as the principal, and including Ray Christian, Chuck Dresser, Grey Dresser, and Bob Laura offered to put money into the corporation, with plans to eventually take ownership.

The LeBus families began backing out of active ownership, but Miller and the others from Oklahoma were unable to consummate a buyout over the next couple of years.

Following that, in 1972, the Arizona-Colorado Land and Cattle Company came on the scene as prospective buyers, offering approximately four million dollars for the properties. This offer was spurned by the LeBus's, but through the ensuing months, the cash hemorrhage continued, with rapidly mounting indebtedness, and a subsequent offer from AZL of approximately two million dollars, plus assumption of existing indebtedness, was accepted.

Ownership was actually vested in a wholly owned subsidiary of AZL, the Baca Grande Angel Fire Corporation. The LeBus family retained 1,000 acres of the old Monte Verde ranch, plus 40 acres west of Agua Fria, located to the north of Hwy. 64, near the base of Palo Flechado Pass.

Therewith, the new owners acquired 22,600 acres on July 26, 1972.

Baca Grande Angel Fire Corporation set about clearing all legitimate indebtedness, which approached six million dollars. Also assumed was the responsibility for installation of utilities to all lot sites, including underground electrical and phone lines. Complicating this commitment, the New Mexico Legislature had just passed a new law, to become effective July 1, 1973, requiring exhaustive feasibility studies, water rights, percolation tests, etc., of all the areas.

Faced with this imperative, AZL brought in another wholly owned subsidiary, the engineering firm of Coe & Van Loo of Phoenix, to immediately "grandfather" in all of the remainder of Country Club Unit I, II, and III, and all of Chalet Units I and II. If the initial building pace of the resort was feverish … activity between October of 1972 and July 1, 1973, was frenzied! Almost all of the platting was done from the air and the task was completed (with the tacit approval of Colfax County officials) by the deadline!

Early in 1973, the Baca Grande Angel Fire Corporation realized the need for a forester. The ski trails were pockmarked with countless big rocks, and the trees cut out for the trails had simply been pushed away from the ski paths into the adjacent trees. Natural fall lines had been disregarded. Trail widths were indiscriminate. Miles of new roads should be built, requiring thousands of trees to be cut.

Stan Samuels, a young employee of the Forest Service, was District Forester in Las Vegas, but had recently been transferred to Ute Park, where he and his wife, Sandra, moved in 1971. In 1973, the Corporation requested Stan to do a resource report, and subsequently employed him from 1973 to 1979. An early assignment was to clear the ski trails of rocks and boulders and remove the trees which had been pushed aside on the trails. As trail manager, he dynamited countless rocks from the trails in 1973 and paid high school boys $100 each to throw the rock fragments off the trails.

Bill Burgess, who ran the ski mountain and ski school from the time the trails were built, estimated that 20,000 skiers visited Angel Fire in 1973. Ernie Blake, who had started the Taos ski area, was recruited to come and help with the Angel Fire ski slopes. After a thorough evaluation, he remarked, "Ye need'ta jack up the mountain a thousand feet and put a wedge under it to make it good and steep!"

Looking from the top of Exhibition run at the Angel Fire Ski Resort, skiers have a virtually unobstructed view of much of Angel Fire and the Moreno Valley. (photo printed with permission of the *Sangre de Cristo Chronicle*)

Within a year, the completion of the Country Club and the Starfire Lodge added much to the luster of the resort. For the grand opening of the Country Club, thousands of square feet of sod were cut and laid for external beautification. Come July 1, 1973, the air was tense with anticipation. All of the women employees were decked out in short, short skirts and white blouses, wearing red, *high* heeled shoes, and badges reading, "May I help you … I'm an Angel!" They were still serving partygoers at 2:00 a.m.

Massive television advertising and mail-outs offering free weekend visits brought hundreds of potential property buyers to the area. A double chair lift was in operation, and the ski trails were being upgraded. Numerous new condominiums were built, and the access roads improved.

Lot sites sold for an average of $5,000 to $10,000, at 10% down, and a ten-year payout at 5% interest. Sales persons could pocket the down payment as commission … a powerful incentive to consummate sales! But … what price success!

A gondola had been ordered from Switzerland, requiring up front payment of half the total cost to get it shipped to a Houston port, but Houston would not release it until the remainder of payment was made. The gondola sat in Houston until it rusted and rotted. The reason? Costs of sales had gradually begun to exceed the proceeds from the sales. There were instances of chicanery, such as the sale of the same lot many times over or selling lots completely unsuitable for building.

So, after pouring millions into the development, AZL Baca Grande pulled out, selling to ProKemCo, who kept the Angel Fire name. Then a subsequent sale of the properties was made to a California company, TosCo Oil, who still retained the name of Angel Fire. Neither of these two buyers were really interested in further development of the resort; their primary interest was in the oil and mineral acquisitions. With the downturn in business in the mid-80s, the properties were again sold, in 1984, to a wealthy bond trader from Little Rock, Arkansas, for $16.5 million. He was Dan Lasater, who later achieved notoriety because of connections to a cocaine ring suspected to be operating with contacts at the Mena, Arkansas airport and thence to the Angel Fire Airport, and was himself convicted of cocaine distribution. Locally, there were also allegations that he had managed to borrow a total of $6 million on six acres of industrial property in Angel Fire. At any rate, imprisonment brought his ownership of the resort to an end.

Dark days lay ahead as the recession of the mid-1980s deepened. New construction came to a virtual standstill. Construction companies dwindled to only a few. Homes, financed by lenders who, earlier, had been eager to provide loans, were deserted when funds for repayment dried up. For both the community and the resort, the deeply intertwined economies suffered.

But one large building project did get its start during Lasater's period of ownership. A developer from Midland, Texas, the Rochester Group, arranged financing to acquire land and begin construction of a new hotel in the ski village. Existing shops, a restaurant, and a bar located near the base lodge were bulldozed away. The total cost was initially estimated to be six million dollars for the completed structure to be called The Plaza.

Major problems were encountered, including partial collapse of one end of the building. Construction costs spiraled, much of which defied usual accountancy, and the final cost reached the incredible amount of $23 million. But finally, in mid-November 1985, the new Plaza Hotel of Angel Fire was ready. It opened with great fanfare, announced by full page newspaper ads, and was ushered in with the "First Annual Calling of the Snow," symbolically imaged with a huge Alpine Horn constructed especially for the opening event. Arnie Jones and Bruce Whitaker, managers of the hotel, initiated a *big* party, and celebrations crescendoed over that whole weekend.

Along with the glittering, auspicious opening of the hotel, an undercurrent of problems began to surface. The owners had insufficient capital to continue the operation. The staff and employees were not getting their promised pay, and unpaid bills were mounting. The following April when the ski season closed, the owners called the lenders and told them, "Pick up the keys, we are without money to operate the hotel." (To this day, most of the principals in the Rochester Group have not been located, though Paul Rochester is known to presently live in Ruidoso under an assumed name; it was the late 1990s before his "bankruptcy" of the hotel was finally discharged.)

It was after the owners' abandonment of the hotel that the second party occurred, a destruction derby type of party! The angry, bilked employees and their friends, after consuming the entire inventory of food and beverage, stripped the hotel of furnishings and equipment, leaving it a shambles. The hotel remained closed and deteriorating for two years and cost nearly $2 million to repair and refurbish. It was then renamed The Legends.

At this juncture, Angel Fire Corporation ownership was taken over by Gary Plante and two others—Evans, and Fagan. Though there was speculation that Lasater still remained the owner, in reality that was never proved. But Plante, Evans and Fagan were successful in pressuring the R.T.C., in whose custody the hotel remained, to sell it to the Corporation, with no money down … and only a pledge for a percentage of the profit to be paid back … (and there was never any profit).

The ensuing decade was characterized as filled with distrust of the owners and management, with the final aggravation of a declaration of bankruptcy. Efforts to bring gambling into the Valley, and with it a new flow of cash, were pursued by Plante, but proved fruitless. The landowners and residents became ensnarled in seemingly endless legal struggles. Finally, in early 1996, the legal questions surrounding the bankruptcy, amenity rights, and ownership dues and other serious areas of dispute were resolved in court to the satisfaction of the individual property owners and the village council. Promising new ownership was assumed by Craig Martin, Tim and Gregg Allen, and a group of limited partners, with reputable financial support. Once again, Angel Fire Resort faced a lustrous and profitable future!

Angel Fire – The Town

As a natural sequence to the progressive development of a beautiful ski, golf, and fishing resort, many who came to play decided to stay. They bought lots, built homes, and some started businesses.

Some of the earliest residents fit the description of pioneers, temporarily living in trailers for makeshift homes, sometimes hauling water, in 50-gallon drums, and depending on deer and elk meat during the lean years.

But that was in the more "recent" Angel Fire era. Others who preceded the LeBus family into the valley also played significant roles in the area's history. Such were the Neals, the Gallaghers, the Witts, the Siementals, the Burks, the Seargeants, and the Bullingtons, among others.

Kay (Witt) Potvin, later a resident of Taos, grew up on the Witt Ranch, also known as the Six-Mile Ranch, which her grandmother had built into a thousand acres, and which stretched south of the Gallagher Ranch. Kay Witt and Billie Burk remember the old log school between Eagle Nest and Agua Fria, where Ruth Seargeant was the teacher. (Kay Moore, a present day resident of Moreno Valley, is Ruth's daughter). Tal Neal and Bill Gallagher were some of Billie's classmates. They also remember at Agua Fria there was a little store, post office, and gas station, called Minnie's Market. There was also a public well, with a pump handle, where passers-by could stop and get some cool water. Minnie's was located at the southeast corner of Hwy 64 and old State Road 38 (now Hwy 434). Billie Burk's father managed the Siemental's ranch, and Billie grew up in the old log house, which still stands on the Camp Elliott Barker Girl Scout campsite.

George LeBus tells the account of Orville Bullington purchasing from the CS Ranch one of the buildings, which would have been inundated by the new Eagle Nest Lake, and moving it ten miles or so to the south. He took it apart, log by log, painting a number on each log. At the new location, he rebuilt the structure, log by numbered log … where it still stands about a mile and a half east of Hwy 434, not far north of town. It was used as the Angel Fire Sportsman's Center. Some of the numbers were still visible on the logs in 1997.

Historic building on Sportsman's Shooting Range, Angel Fire. Originally on the site of Eagle Nest Lake, each log was numbered, dismantled, and moved to the present location before the dam was completed. (Photo by Martin Andrews)

Descendants of the Neals and Gallaghers continue to live in this area.

Along with supplies and workers, the LeBus family brought a number of trailers for temporary homes for supervisors and employees. Later, as some of those workers moved on, the trailers were purchased for temporary dwellings by some of the earliest "new" pioneers of the valley. Such was Bets Loving, who made her first visit to Angel Fire along with a friend, Margaret Jamison, owner of an art gallery in Santa Fe. That was in 1966 and Bets thought Angel Fire was the most beautiful place she had ever seen. "I saw it and I loved it. I paid down on a lot and on a commercial property. I, later on, moved my family here in 1967, into a trailer vacated by an engineer who had helped build the ski area."

Bets and her brother-in-law ran the base lodge in the back basin, doing double shifts much of the time, along with Pauline May and her husband. (When AZL took ownership in 1972, Bets was asked to stay on in their sales department.)

Not a great amount of snow fell in 1967, the first year of the new resort.

George LeBus says of that year, "Our snow makin' machine was five dump trucks, loadin' up with snow from down at the blinkin' light and haulin' it up to the base and fishin' it up the slopes!"

Then the winter of 1968 started disastrously for an up-and-coming ski resort ... hardly a flake of snow had fallen. Workers abandoned the ski slopes and the whole area emptied out. And it was bitterly cold. Water pipes for the trailers froze, necessitating hauling water from Eagle Nest.

Bets Loving said, "I found that my family could get by on 13 gallons of water a day for drinking, cooking, and washing!"

Russ Sylvester, an engineer in Cleveland, Ohio, was invited by his fiancée, Kay, to come to Angel Fire in February of that year. Kay, an artist, had visited Taos the year before, and had then come to Angel Fire, purchased a condo, and moved into it. All were bemoaning the lack of snow and hoping for a miracle. Russ recalls, "The afternoon I was to leave, the clouds gathered, and it became apparent that snow was on its way. Then everybody went up to the base lodge and 'had a drink for every snowflake that fell.' It was a wild night!"

Russ and Kay were married the following June, honeymooned here, and Russ moved his business to Angel Fire, building their home a short time later. Russ would later become the first president of the Southern Moreno Valley Community Corporation. He was an E.M.T. for 15 years and was on the Search and Rescue team for two years.

By the year 1970, there were five homes built in Angel Fire. Navy Captain George Block and his wife bought a lot in 1968, built a house in 1969 and, upon retiring in 1970, he and Betsy moved here.

The Cardwells had been the first to construct a home. The Elys and the McQuarries were others. But with the infusion of money and zeal by Baca Grande came a great influx of home building and by June 1973, the number reached twenty-five with an expected fifteen more before the year end. In 1974, the number of homes built and under construction approached ninety. Steady growth was virtually certain to continue, and with that population increase would come the need for goods and services to be provided locally, including security, health care, fire protection, churches, restaurants, mail service, and stores.

In the summer of 1972, a trio of men making a trip from Amarillo to Taos, then swinging back through Angel Fire were affected by the beauty of the area and by the planned resort sufficiently enough to persuade them to buy some commercial property. The trio consisted of Jerry Hodge, Geary Taylor, and Joe Don Looney (the Looney of dubious football fame … Oklahoma Sooners and later several pro teams). They, along with others in Amarillo, had formed an investment group. They had been college roommates and had made the trip to Taos at the suggestion of Looney, to visit a "hippie commune." Jerry also bought a lot and later built a home in Angel Fire.

James Butts, also of Amarillo, and a friend of these men, had become a pharmacist and at that time was working in a pharmacy in Odessa, Texas. But in the summers of 1968 and 1969 he had worked as a ranger and then as a training ranger at the Philmont Scout Center, under the supervision of Buzz Clemmons. (Clemmons later retired from Philmont and moved to Angel Fire where he became active as a businessman until his death in 1995).

Hodge and Taylor left Looney at the "hippie commune." The combination of Hodge, Taylor, and James Butts, with the purchase of commercial land here, proved to be a signal event. In 1974 Hodge, Taylor and twenty other investors formed a corporation and built the original Mini-Mart, a convenience store and gas station, which was the first business in Angel Fire. However, trying to manage the business long distance was distressing to the group and they were realizing a very marginal profit. Hodge convinced James Butts to leave his job in Odessa, Texas and become the manager of the Mini-Mart. James made the move on the condition that a space for a pharmacy would be added.

The deal was a wise one for the owners and a good one for Butts. Business began to thrive, and within a decade, Butts, Hodge, and Bob Bauman bought out the remaining investors, becoming partners in the Mini-Mart Plaza complex, providing space for other business enterprises, and for municipal offices. Butts earned prominence in the developing community. He initially served on the Board of the Eagle Nest-Angel Fire Chamber of Commerce, of the Southern Moreno Valley Community Corporation, the Search and Rescue Team, and the Angel Fire Chamber of Commerce, all before being elected as the first mayor of Angel Fire.

In a growing community, nothing happens in an isolated way. As the "business district" came into being, and sales and services multiplied, knowledgeable residents realized that a lot of tax money was being collected and sent off to county and state agencies, but that little or none was being returned. The remedy: incorporation as a municipality.

It was not long before a committee formed to begin a serious study of the intricacies of incorporation. Stanton Bundy and Al Lopez co-chaired the group. George Block represented the Property Owners Association (the group to whom the facilities might eventually be transferred). Don Borgeson represented the Angel Fire Chamber of Commerce (Executive Director). Barbara Hopper represented the Community Corporation and Chris Jacobson represented the Angel Fire Corporation. Russ Sylvester also was a member.

The process was slow. State statutes required a population density of one person per acre of anticipated incorporated area, with the further requirement of at least 150 people living in the area. Owners of at least sixty percent of the acreage within the proposed incorporated area had to sign the petition. All requirements were fulfilled, but only by gerrymandering 186 residents into an area of 168 acres. As much commercial property was included as possible in order to maximize return of gross receipts taxes to the community. Finally, a majority vote of all qualified voters was necessary. By a vote of 44 to 16, voters chose to incorporate.

On April 8, 1986, the first election of the soon-to-be 99th New Mexico municipality was held. The results (57 voted):

For Mayor: James Butts (unopposed) 57 votes

For Council:

David Ambrose 53 votes

Don Loscerbo 43 votes

Bill Diveley 42 votes

Alan Sebesta 31 votes

Christine Herlihy 31 votes

For Judge: Vickie Hudson 41 votes

State statutes required that, in a municipal election, any tie vote must be decided by a game of chance or by lot. Thus, to break the tie between Sebesta and Herlihy, Mayor Butts went to the county courthouse in Raton and in the County Clerk's office, for all the world to see ... he dealt a hand of five card stud. Alan Sebesta had high hand. The event drew coverage in the *Albuquerque Journal*, the *Raton Range*, *The Taos News*, other newspapers, and national television.

Butts and the council members served the first year without remuneration. Law stipulated that no elected official's salary could be raised during their term of office. But going from nothing to something was not a raise. Frank Coppler, an attorney, gave free advice on this matter.

"No elected city official could receive a salary higher than that of a county commissioner." Butts's salary was then set at $550 per month, and salaries for the council members and the judge at 60% of the amount. It would be three years later, in 1989, before the first Police Chief, Bill Conley, would be employed.

But for the newest New Mexico municipality of Angel Fire Village, the day it became a legal entity was July 1, 1986. Governor Toney Anaya proclaimed that day *Angel Fire Day*. It was ironic that the prime movers in the labor of incorporation could not vote on the issue, nor could they be eligible for office, because their own homesites were located outside the gerrymandered areas.

Optimism and exuberance marked the years following 1972. Baca Grande Angel Fire Corporation had contracted with Habitat, a Phoenix firm specializing in design and marketing aids for developing businesses. One of their talented young employees, Mike Laverty, was a designer and graphic artist, and was assigned to work on the Angel Fire contract. From sales office design, to logos and landmark outdoor signs, Mike and others produced and fabricated two big trailer loads of promotional materials and signs, hauled them from Phoenix to Angel Fire, and constructed them here. Mike fell in love with the beauty of the valley (and in love with a girl he met here) and decided to move here. He helped Gil Jones design and build some of the early condominiums, built the pharmacy addition onto the original Mini-Mart, helped construct the Visitor's Center at the Vietnam Memorial, and later designed and built homes. The long-familiar signs, made of peeled logs, slanting upward to frame redwood panels with white raised lettering, ANGEL FIRE, and stone work beneath, were designed and constructed by him.

Bob Bright, a Missourian retired from the Department of Conservation and, following that, the developer and owner of a marina on Table Rock Lake in the Ozarks, came to Raton, New Mexico, in 1973 to visit his sister and nephew. He had sold the marina and was undecided as yet where he would move in retirement. His nephew persuaded him to visit Angel Fire and he liked what he saw. At the same time, he recognized a need for conservation expertise in the ongoing development of the resort area.

Bright approached the corporation with an offer to provide a study and report and was immediately retained. He was also respected for his salesmanship and was subsequently asked to join the sales force. Successful at that, he was sent to real estate school and afterward was in charge of the real estate salespeople for the corporation. On May 1, 1976, he and Bets Loving established the Monte Verde Realty Company, which was the second real estate company in Angel Fire to handle re-sales (Orchard Realty was the first). Bob's to-be wife, Gertie, came to his real estate office looking for a homesite and ended up with a choice husband and home!

It is axiomatic that an increasing population and a growing business environment brings with it an awareness and concern for the more mundane essentials of community and culture—fire and police protection, access to medical care, places of worship, library facilities and a modicum of the arts. There was an additional concern, especially acute for the property and landowners, that the Property Owners Association (P.O.A.) was not a suitable organization to represent them in case of real dispute or conflict with the Angel Fire Corporation. Indeed, the P.O.A. was dormant. And again, two stalwarts, Jock McQuarrie and George Block, began the formation of HALO (Home and Land Owners), to function as a watch dog organization with the purpose and ability to pursue all legal remedies necessary for the protection of home and land owner rights. George served as the first president of HALO, followed by Jock, then Stanton Bundy, Burt Sheff (during one of the most confrontational times with the Corporation), and Don Loscerbo during the early years.

In 1974, before any kind of medical care was available in Angel Fire, a prominent part-time resident, Jack Stromberg, sustained a heart attack which proved to be fatal before distant ambulance service could be obtained. A friend and fellow citizen, C.R. "Bits" Hoover, was dismayed and vowed to do something to remedy such a problem. "Bits," as he was usually called, went to a used-ambulance dealer in the Texas panhandle and purchased two station wagon ambulances and brought them back to Angel Fire, keeping one for the town and allowing the other to be used by the Corporation. His son, Tommy, was an Emergency Medical Technician, and he sparked the development of the Angel Fire Emergency Service.

Volunteers were quickly trained to serve as ambulance drivers and EMTs. Among them were Bob Lasseter, Martha Lasseter, Burt Sheff, George Block, Betty Harney, Al and Dot Harney, Larry Holtz, Mary and Stan Painter, Lisa Rollins, Sue Vestal, Bob Cofield (a retired orthopedic surgeon), Carolyn Granger and Jeanne Cheatham.

The first modern ambulance was later purchased by the Southern Moreno Valley Community Corporation, which was the umbrella organization for the emergency medical services: the fire station, the search and rescue team, and the library. Land was donated for a building to house these facilities by the Angel Fire Corporation, which also paid for half of the cost of building the fire station, with the stipulation that the property would revert back to the Corporation in the event other uses of the building occurred in the future.

Glen "Poopsie" Miller and Tom Sabus were credited with getting the fire station built. Tom, who had been a fireman in Phoenix, became the first

Fire Chief and Bill Burgess was assistant chief. Glen and Tom arranged financing for the building from a banker in Springer, New Mexico, and they both personally signed the mortgage. After the Community Corporation was fully formed and operational it assumed the mortgage. A modern fire engine was purchased and the cost of that, in part, was paid by State Fire Marshal funding with the balance financed by Springer banker, Bob Nex, who loved to golf at Angel Fire. The Stromberg family, prominent Albuquerque merchants, made generous contributions to the fire station and helped raise money to pay it off. (Tragically, their Angel Fire home was destroyed by fire the year following Jack's death.) The name, Stromberg Center, honors the family.

With the impetus of trained EMTs, ambulance drivers, and some available space in the Stromberg Center, two physicians from Taos, Dr. Pond and Dr. Rosen, along with a physician's assistant came to Angel Fire to hold clinic three days a week. That began in 1977 and provided for many of the acute and more easily managed chronic care needs of the growing population.

Following Doctors Pond and Rosen came a much respected physician, Dr. Bob Gordon. Although his practice was in Raton, he spent regular clinic time in Angel Fire and eventually made his home here. He later moved a double-wide mobile home into Angel Fire, equipping it to function as a medical office and calling it the Moreno Valley Health Care Clinic. He gradually spent more time in Angel Fire and less in Raton, continuing much needed services in the southern Moreno Valley. Following Dr. Gordon's retirement, operation of the clinic was assumed by the Southern Colfax County Special Hospital District and another physician was successfully recruited. Dr. Dennis Cohen practiced in the same temporary building until finally a modern clinic facility was completed in early 1996.

Security and law enforcement began, locally, when the Baca Grande Angel Fire Corporation hired John Schotanus to patrol all of the corporate property. He would also, by separate contract, patrol for private property owners. It is said that he developed agoraphobia, becoming unable to perform daytime duties at all. He later sold out to Richard Hill who continued to operate the Northern New Mexico Security Service.

Archie Borrunda was temporarily employed by the village as a policeman. Full-time police service began in 1989, with the appointment of Bill Conley as Chief of Police.

In addition to his official position, Chief Conley was also frequently involved in search and rescue efforts. Larry Holtz, who was a volunteer EMT and fireman as well as a state coordinator for the New Mexico Search and Rescue Department had, for several years, responded to urgent calls for search and rescue by rounding up locals who would agree to help him. It is said that some of these volunteers may have imbibed sufficiently to adversely affect proper search and rescue measures and would, themselves, become lost and need to be rescued.

Eventually Chief Conley and twenty-three local citizens incorporated, through the State Department of Public Safety, as a local Search and Rescue Chapter, a non-profit organization. In addition to annual dues, AFSAR receives a small sum each year from the Community Corporation and manages to realize some money from fundraiser events. The team responds to local needs as well as those outside the area. Volunteers maintain skills by attending training sessions monthly, at Philmont, Red River and Taos. They pay all their own expenses. The team responds to calls on an average of once a month.

Opportunities for church attendance and worship were limited in the formative years of Angel Fire. In the early 1980s an Angel Fire Baptist fellowship was formed and met regularly for a while. Later, as others of different denominational background attended, the name was changed to Angel Fire Community Church. For a number of reasons, this group eventually disbanded.

However, the Baptist members of the group, through a relationship with the large First Baptist Church of Dallas, Texas, were able to forge a sponsorship from that church as a mission. The Angel Fire Corporation donated land for a building site and in 1984 construction was begun. The excavation, grading and foundation work was done by Samuels Construction, after which the building was rapidly completed, largely by volunteer crews from other Baptist churches and local members. The Rev. Dann Masters ably served as pastor for the church for a number of years, during which time the church earned an enviable position in the community.

Qualifying as the "oldest" church in Angel Fire, Christ Our Savior Lutheran Church (Missouri Synod) has held continuous, regular worship services since 1984. The congregation met in the upper level of the Stromberg Center. The Rev. Mr. George Putnam served as pastor for the first year, then a lay pastor, Mr. Carl Fisher from Santa Fe, served the congregation until 1993. In the summer of 1994, the Rev. Mr. Charles Keogh assumed pastoral leadership. Enthusiasm ran high for the members as they completed their new church building on acreage just west of the Moreno Valley Health Care Clinic.

In 1989, a group of Presbyterians began organizing for worship, study, and fellowship. Dr. A.L. Hoermann and his wife, Wanda, were the initiators with Dr. Hoermann acting as convener. Soon thereafter, the Rev. Mr. John Snider, a retired chaplain, and the pastor of Taos Presbyterian Church, supplied pastoral care and preaching for one and a half years.

Following Rev. Snider, the Rev. Mr. Andy McComb served as pastor for another year and a half. During his tenure, the group grew to include people of several other denominational backgrounds, especially United Methodists, Disciples of Christ, Church of the Brethren, United Church of Christ, Episcopal, the Evangelical Lutheran Church in America, and Roman Catholic members. McComb contacted Wallace Ford of the New Mexico Council of Churches, who suggested formation of a multi-denominational ecumenical congregation, patterned after the Consultation on Church Union.

Subsequently, the Disciples of Christ, the Presbyterian, and the United Methodist Churches agreed to join in underwriting initial funding for the new United Church of Angel Fire and the church was incorporated in June 1994. The first full-time pastor, the Rev. Dr. Tracey Miller, came in January 1995.

The church experienced rapid growth and moved into a remarkably beautiful building, completed in June 1999, located on West Ridge Road, west of Highway 434. Christmas Eve services held at the Legends Hotel for three years were highlights for the congregation. The church also hosted a Seder each year, led by Rabbi Chavah Carp of B Nai Shalom Havurah in Taos. The church was officially chartered on July 28, 1996, when dignitaries from the Presbyterian, Disciples of Christ, and United Methodist denominations were present. Although Dr. Miller holds ordination from the Disciples of Christ, that ordination is fully recognized by the other participating church bodies.

As far back as 1982, though commercial building had been proceeding steadily on the east side of the road leading into Angel Fire, little had developed on the west side. But, in a circuitous way, that was about to change.

For some time, the need to enlarge the airport and to get a fixed-base operator in place had been recognized. All of this required significant expense and land. Guy Lanon, retired from the F.A.A., was instrumental in getting matching funds to accomplish this. In a roundabout way, here is how it happened:

The Amarillo investment group (with the business name, "Devil Oil") who had built the original Mini-Mart, also owned land which would be needed for airport expansion. The County was required to come up with a match of funds, which the F.A.A. would provide. A deal was worked out whereby that site was deeded back to Angel Fire Corporation in exchange for a different parcel of land, the site where the Village Hall and a bank building are currently located in 2021. The Angel Fire Corporation then gave back that acquired site, along with much more acreage to Colfax County, land which the county then used as its percentage match of the Federal funds. The airport expansion progressed, and Pierce Aviation came on the scene as the fixed-base operator. Angel Fire could then boast the fifth highest airport in the continental US at 8,382 feet and a runway of 8,900 by 100 feet.

So it was that in 1982, construction of a business strip was begun on the west side of Angel Fire's main road. C.R. "Bits" Hoover, a distributor and jobber for Phillips Petroleum in Pampa, Texas, built the Centro Plaza building. In addition, he built the Village Restaurant uphill west of the south end of the Plaza and five stucco houses west of the restaurant. The restaurant was not successful. The Hoovers also built a lovely stucco home in Angel Fire.

There is a poignant story about Bits' son Tommy and his dog, Kilo. The dog was a huge St. Bernard and theirs was a special kind of friendship. (The name Kilo refers to the pup's birthweight.) Kilo was always in Tommy's big ol' Suburban and the vehicle was painted the very same colors as the dog. He always waited in the car while Tommy went about his errands and even when he went skiing. Everybody knew Kilo, even the license plate read KILO.

Then Kilo died. Tommy took a Caterpillar, excavated a big grave on the crest of the hill west of the small house next to the restaurant, put Kilo in the Suburban, and drove the Suburban into the hole. He then covered it over with dirt, leaving only the tip of the antenna above the ground!

Within a year after the building of Centro Plaza in the spring of 1983, Angel Fire got its first "real" grocery, produce, and meat market. Located on the east side of the main road at the intersection of North Angel Fire Road and the highway, the store was built and operated by Dick Railsback, who called it the Valley Market. It was under his ownership until the spring of 1991 when it was purchased by Charlie and Jean Robison. A bakery, smoked meat specialties, and gasoline station, plus video rentals, added to the products and services provided by the market. The Robisons sold the Valley Market to the Lowe's grocery chain in the mid-2000s.

In all communities, sooner or later everyone wants to learn all they can about everybody and everything and to keep current with newsworthy events. And although the *Albuquerque Journal* and the *Taos News* were available, the news was usually not local enough to satisfy the growing population of Angel Fire. Still, it would not be until six years after the resort was built the first newspaper hit the streets.

In 1973, Joe Gallagher began publishing two newspapers: *The Red River Prospector* and *The Moreno Valley Lantern*. The first issues came out in July of that year and continued, on a bimonthly schedule, for a period of two years. Joe then merged the two papers into the *Sangre de Cristo Chronicle* in June 1975, continuing on a bimonthly schedule.

The *Chronicle* was purchased in 1984 by Guy and Marcia Wood and continued publishing weekly until the couple retired. The owner of the *Taos News* took over in 2006, but ceased distribution in November 2015, and Ellen Miller Goins, a former reporter for the *Chronicle* kept an online edition active for some years. In 2020, the *Blinking Light Newspaper* realized a need and began publishing a print edition of news for Angel Fire and the Enchanted Circle area.

To be able to send and receive mail regularly and easily was another community need. Mail was delivered with reasonable regularity to Star Route rural boxes, but the new Angel Fire residents had to travel to the Eagle Nest Post Office. The first local mail service was a makeshift branch office opened in the former coat-check room at the Angel Fire Country Club. E.O. "Buzz" Clemmons was the first postmaster. Soon, the Angel Fire Post Office became a full-time contract station, operated as a branch of the Eagle Nest Post Office. Still, there were frequent changes in who would run the contract station, which entailed a change of location every year or two. In the mid-2000s, the village and residents petitioned the US Postal Service to make Angel Fire's branch a real, official post office. The petition was granted, and it operates as such today.

Fishing, golfing, hiking, and skiing all produce a good appetite and sufficient fatigue to warrant "eating out." So, in 1967, the initial year of Angel Fire skiing and golfing, food service became available at the base lodge, and later in the back basin warming hut, catering to the ski crowd.

When the country club opened in 1973 it boasted a posh restaurant, plus live music. In 1975, Homer and Minnie Steen opened "Steens," a restaurant. Texas Red's occupied a large building nearby, specializing in steaks, from 1974 to 1975 when it was closed. Subsequently it reopened as the Stage Stop in June 1976 and went through a series of operators until it was torn down to allow construction of the Plaza Hotel.

After the hotel was restored and reopened as the Legends, two new in-hotel restaurants opened: the "Mill," serving breakfast and lunch and "Springer's" for fine evening dining. Additionally, "Annie O's" provided a full-service bar and video entertainment. The new ownership of the resort has brought with it a renaming of the hotel, the restaurants, and the bar, with the hotel now known as Angel Fire Resort Hotel.

For the convenience of golfers, but open to the public as well, the

"19th Hole" adjacent to the Pro Shop was available.

A brief trip down memory lane regarding other Angel Fire restaurants that date back to prior to 1997 include: "Annie's Hitching Post – Saloon and Bar" (site of present "Zeb's") was born in November 1984 but died in June 1985. Acquired by Rocky Thompson of Farmington, New Mexico, it became known as "Zebediah's Restaurant and Pub" in 1985 and was managed by Sam Macias, who later bought the establishment.

At the site of the original Mini-Mart, an early eatery was known as the "Feed Bin." It was later enlarged to house the "Golden Nugget" in 1989. In 1991 it was purchased and renovated by Deana Olguin and renamed "Coyote Creek Café," (now the site of the Sweet Shirt Co.). Other well-known restaurants included "Pizza Stop," "Rocky Mountain BBQ and Grill," and "Tres Amigos" in the Elk Horn Lodge.

Some good restaurants that somehow didn't last were Aldo's Lift, Herman's (in Redwood Common – later became The Tavern), Bandanna's, and the Commons Club (in Pinetree Commons).

Over the years, many of the abovementioned restaurants came and went. Angel Fire is a town of constant movement, and new offerings come along so it is impossible to present any type of current-day listing. Find whatever is here now—and enjoy!

As commerce and construction advanced along with the growth of the resort, the need for local banking services also grew. The Sunwest Bank (subsequently NationsBank, then Bank of America, then Washington Federal) was the first branch bank in Angel Fire, followed shortly, thereafter, by the International State Bank (later, International Bank, then INBank). The 1990s and early 2000s saw major new commercial enterprises such as the Elk Horn Lodge built by Bill and Nancy Burch, also known for their Roadrunner Tours business. The Pinewood Plaza buildings, the Houston Ace Hardware and RBS True Value Hardware, along with other planned commercial and office buildings have changed the face of the Village.

In concert with financial services of the banks, several real estate agencies, in addition to the early Angel Fire Resort Properties, provided expertise in the purchasing, sale and trading of real properties. Among the first in Angel Fire were Orchard Realty, Monte Verde Realty, North Country Real Estate, Bush Realtors, Sun Valle Realty and Granger Realty. More recent are offices affiliated with nationally known names such as RE/Max, Coldwell Banker, Keller Williams, and more.

A very unique and beautiful close neighbor to Angel Fire is the regional camp area of the Girl Scout Council, Camp Elliott Barker. This particular Council region encompasses thirteen counties in northeastern New Mexico plus Las Animas County in Colorado.

The camp is located on 536 acres to the west and north of the village, at the base of a mountain where the timbered area merges into the open south end of the Moreno Valley. It is remarkably well adapted to the development of facilities required for such a camp. One of the oldest, if not truly the oldest of log houses in the valley still stands in good repair on the campsite. An old barn also remains in good condition.

The land, owned in the 1950s by George and Ann Siemental, later came into the possession of Mary Anne Sweikhardt, from whom it was purchased by the Scout Council in December 1962. The Council retained Mr. Elliott Barker, the respected forester and hunter (who rescued a bear cub from being burned in a forest fire and named the bear Smokey, creating the famous "Smokey the Bear" campaign) to assess a half dozen different possible camp sites and make recommendation as to the best area.

He was unequivocal in his choice, stating: "Over a period of two years I have looked at many tracts for the Girl Scout Council and have seen none that have the desirable attributes and potentials for an unusually fine camp site that exist here."

Barker came to this part of the country in 1893 at the age of three and died at the age of 103! Honoring him, the camp was named Camp Elliott Barker in 1975, having been called simply "the Girl Scout Camp near Eagle Nest" during the first fifteen years of operation. According to Alice Ewing, historian for the Council, the land was bought from proceeds from the sale of Girl Scout cookies! The American Camping Association, which is an independent accrediting program, reviews camp operations all over the country, focusing on health and safety aspects and program quality of camps. Camp Elliott Barker receives full accreditation from the A.C.A.

* * *

The cultural aspirations and needs of Angel Fire have been met, at least in part, by a wide range of motivated, energetic, and talented residents, some part-timers and some permanent.

In 1978, Jeanette Stromberg and Martha Lassetter spear-headed the formation of a library, located originally in the country club building, creating a valuable asset for the village and the area. Later, Ruth Lawrence and many others combined efforts to steadily improve the library.

In 1999, the library developed computer capability to become interactive with other libraries on-line and kicked off a capital fund campaign to enlarge the library facility. The computer equipment was a gift from the Gates Foundation, the Southern Moreno Valley Community Corporation provided space for the library in the Stromberg Center building. Ruth Lawrence, then-president of the Library Board, welcomed more volunteers so that the library could remain open more hours per week. The other members of the board were Martha Lassetter, Jan Lassetter, Debbie Clanton, Jan Jones, Isabella Neff, Joan Salas, and Susan Vaughn. All served without pay, as do additional volunteers.

Soon, the library was rapidly outgrowing its space in the Stromberg Center building, so the ladies once again went into action. Massive fundraising efforts were initiated. Angel Fire Resort donated a parcel of land at the intersection of North Angel Fire Road and South Angel Fire Road, and Shuter Construction agreed to build the building at cost. The community pitched in and raised enough money, and the Shuter Library of Angel Fire opened its doors in July 2002. It operates as a 501(c) 3 nonprofit entity and is supported by local businesses, donations, grants, and fundraisers. The Shuter Library hosts many book-related community events for kids and adults and also showcases the efforts of local authors.

The Moreno Valley Writers Guild formed in 1991 under the umbrella of the Moreno Valley Arts Council. This active writer's group provided opportunities for both established and budding authors to develop their skills. Outstanding workshops sponsored by the Guild brought a wide range of authors, editors, and publishers to Angel Fire. The Guild also sponsored annual contests for aspiring youth and adult writers, and published several anthologies of its members' work, along with *Lure, Lore, and Legends*, this history of the Moreno Valley, and a volume called *Enchanted Adventures: Diverse Day Trips in Northern New Mexico*. Membership was robust during the 1990s and 2000s, but began to decline in the 2010s. The Guild was officially disbanded in September 2011, and the remaining money in its treasury donated to the Shuter Library.

For the hardy and outdoor type, the Moreno Valley Trekker's Club schedules walking and hiking trips and encourages continuing study of the flora and fauna of the valley and surrounding high places. Club members also spent much time cutting a trail thirty miles long over Osha Pass and mountain, Apache Pass, Cerro Vista, and Tres Ritos, to connect with walking trails on down to Santa Fe.

An active Angel Fire Garden Club was responsible for much of the flowering beauty seen around so many homes and the orderly array of wildflowers in some areas. The club had its early start in the mid-1970s, when Betsy Block, Dot Harney, Joan LeBus, Nadine Ashcraft, Jane Miller, Nancy Burge, Marian Clemmons and several others joined together to form the first serious beginning. Each Christmas season, these women decorated the Country Club with wreaths and uprights and ropes of fresh-cut greenery and a large beautifully decorated Christmas tree. But in time, with the changing of ownership of the resort, this initial group became inactive.

A few years later, however, in 1989, Sidney Burgess approached Kathy Kalen to discuss the need to establish an active Garden Club. Betty Ann Moon and many others of the original group joined the effort. In 1991, Betty Picquet was of great assistance in the reorganization of the club, which by that time numbered 36 members, and together they founded the Angel Fire Garden Club, and federated with the National Garden Club. Betty Ann Moon served as the first president, 1991-1993.

Their contributions to the overall beauty of our community have been substantial, and include the lovely medians of flowers, trees, and shrubs along the boulevard portion of North Angel Fire Road, the provision of wooden flower boxes (built by Al Sindel) which adorn local places of business, along with initial flower plantings in these boxes. Each year at the Christmas season, the club supplied the special lighting for a large Christmas tree, along with free refreshments, on the festive evening at the first lighting of the tree. This was a tradition at the corner of Mountain View Boulevard and North Angel Fire Road until the completion of the new Community Center. The club has participated in the cost of a new tree at the Community Center and plans to carry on this tradition there each year. The club also takes responsibility for keeping a one-mile section of Highway 434 free of trash and debris. Of interest to almost everyone in the valley, is the publication of *Nature Has Its Way*, the club's book on gardening in the southern Rocky Mountains.

Old-timers remember when, in the early 1980s, the original "Balloons Over Angel Fire" mid-summer event started, but fewer may recall that it was really begun by Phyllis McGuire, a real estate broker, who had started piloting and owning hot air balloons while living in Albuquerque. Increasingly, the hot-air balloon event has attracted up to 60 participants, all vying for the most colorful, highest, and smoothest flights and neatest landings. In 1995, the extravaganza was expanded and given a new name, "Wings Over Angel Fire," with activities at the airport which included helicopter rides, bi-plane, glider and radio-controlled airplane show, planetarium shows and a birds of prey special presentation. Recent years have seen somewhat scaled-back versions of the event, but balloons return each summer to delight residents and visitors alike.

On the cultural side, a serene summer event was the Summer Music Conservatory featuring faculty and student chamber music concerts.

In 1983, A.R.T.S. (acronym for Angel Fire Repertory Theater Society) began productions of seven plays each year, in many different venues, including the Village Haus, a summer-time big yellow tent in the lower ski parking area, and in under-utilized space in the Centro Plaza. The A.R.T.S. was the result of the efforts of many, but the dynamic trio who made it succeed were Carolyn and William Granger and Jimmy Linton. For a number of years, their productions were widely anticipated and well received by locals and visitors. And though currently inactive, plans have been discussed to fund and build a center for cultural and performing arts.

In the 1990s, the Grangers and Jimmy Linton, along with "Sam" Tietze, Pam Coleman, and Frances Marsalis began, as an outgrowth of A.R.T.S., the Moreno Valley Arts Council, which staged an extremely popular "ArtsFest" annually.

Another jewel in the Village's crown is Music From Angel Fire (MFAF). Featuring world famous artists with concert venues in Angel Fire, Taos, Raton, Las Vegas, and Santa Fe, and a special venue in Angel Fire with an Art Auction Benefit and a gala dinner, MFAF has consistently gained support from an appreciative New Mexico audience. Those who envisioned such a grand cultural accomplishment and have worked diligently to make it happen and keep it going include Harold Geller, owner of Total Arts Gallery in Taos, and Leonard Altman, a Californian, both of whom served as the first two presidents of the organization. An outgrowth of the New Mexico Festival of Music (Taos) which had been in existence five years, Music From Angel Fire inaugurated its premiere season in 1984. In 1985 Ida Kavafian was hired as music director and a new executive director, John Giovando, of the Santa Fe Chamber Music Festival, was employed. Together they set the festival in a higher direction, drawing many musicians of renown to MFAF.

Vital to the success of MFAF were many residents of Angel Fire including Chuck Horne (then president of Angel Fire Corporation), Max and Nancy Mertz, Lois Reidy, Jerry Halpern, Ron May, Phyllis McGuire, Al and Lil Sindel, Bob and Ginny Ely, Norm and Sam Tietze, Pam Coleman, and Don Borgeson. George Houston (Houston Lumber Co.) was a strong financial contributor. Curt Keeler of Sunwest Bank assisted with financing. The highly successful Music from Angel Fire Posters idea was inspired by Harold Geller. Jackie Erwin, Jack and Shirley Douglass, and Beck and Robyn Atkinson were others deeply involved in the success of the organization.

Added to ensure success financially, MFAF established the Margaret Fowler Endowment Trust with a generous bequest at Margaret Fowler's death. She was a resident of Taos.

A delightful and easily perceptible characteristic of the great majority of Angel Fire residents is that they are here by *choice*. Not coerced by forced job relocation nor persuaded against their will or better judgment, they are simply drawn by the lure and irresistible beauty of the Moreno Valley. That happened in the case of the very early valley residents and keeps on motivating others to make the valley their home. It also happened to Ruth Bush who was a Realtor in Houston, Texas, and her husband.

Back in the fall of 1978 after years of living and working in Houston, they decided to begin looking for a less congested, cooler location where her husband could begin a general contracting business and she could continue her work in real estate. They traveled to several smaller cities and towns farther north in Texas in search of the right place, but mostly met frustration.

Then, as Ruth vividly recalled, "Out of the blue an acquaintance called and said, 'You ought to go up and see a place called Angel Fire! It is the most beautiful place we have ever seen, and it is a planned community which would just suit all you've been looking for.'"

A subsequent trip from Houston to Angel Fire was all it took to convince them. By April 1979, they had liquidated their assets in Houston and moved to Angel Fire, eager to become a part of the community and to establish Bush Realtors and the general contracting business. Ruth also became active and supportive in the activities surrounding incorporation of the village and later in its governance. Subsequently she would be selected by the Village Council as mayor in 1991 at a time when both the mayor and the mayor pro tem resigned due to changes in residence. And it was during her term of office that the beautiful North Angel Fire Road widening, and sidewalk construction project was accomplished. Although initially opposed by many, completion of the project brought general acclaim.

Ruth Bush, along with mayor Barbara Cottam, many former and present council members, business leaders, clergy, and concerned citizens shared a recognition of real needs yet to be met as Angel Fire continued to grow: adequate low-cost housing, schools, and increased medical facilities.

Other legislative priorities would bring funding for several community needs, including construction of a new wastewater facility (completed in 1999), continued funding for a tourism office, increased funds for fire and police facilities, continued highway improvement for northern New Mexico, and for the purchase of water rights to meet a 100-year projected need.

A large new Community Center was completed. Mayor Cottam rightly designates this functional and beautiful building as the most significant legacy of her two terms as mayor.

Attracting younger families to Angel Fire required better options for schooling. Grades K-8 attended school in Eagle Nest, a bus ride of only 10 miles, but for those in high school, it was 36 miles of winding mountain road to Cimarron, in less than ideal conditions in the winter. A group of parents and dedicated Angel Fire citizens decided to pursue a better answer. Much research into curriculum and diligent work went into founding a charter school, to be located in Angel Fire, and in 2001 the Moreno Valley High School was the first Paideia-based high school in New Mexico. It remains one of the only high schools totally based in Paideia methodology. Moreno Valley High School is nationally ranked by both the *Washington Post* Challenge Index and by *U.S. News & World Report* and has been designated as a Gold Medal School.

Angel Fire, the 99th and newest municipality in New Mexico, is still young and its roots in the Valley scarcely measure fifty years! Doubtless, few, if any, communities across the country can match its beauty, its enviable progress, and its clear vision for the future.

* * *

Martin Andrews, a native Missourian, moved to Kansas at age 17, where he pursued undergraduate and graduate medical education, interrupted by World War II service in the Signal Corps. He received his M.D. degree from the University of Kansas in 1952 and practiced family medicine for 42 years in Oklahoma City before retiring in 1995. He and his wife, Phillis, first came to the valley in 1974 and purchased land for a home in 1975. They became full time residents of Angel Fire in June 1995 and he became a member of the Moreno Valley Writer's Guild.

Black Lake

by Jack C. Urban

Immediately south of the Moreno Valley, along Highway 434, is a ranching and farming community known as Black Lake or in Spanish, Laguna Negra. It has changed little since it was first homesteaded by Spanish Mexicans in the 1880s. Yet its history mirrors an interesting and important contrast to its Moreno Valley counterparts. Because it was not a part of the Maxwell Land Grant, it was spared direct involvement in the Colfax County War.

The southern boundaries of the grant can be defined by a hill south of Angel Fire called El Bordo. Continuing south, a narrow meadow expands to become a valley to the west, separating at the junction of highways 434 and 120. To the right is the dominant feature of the area, a large pond nestled at the base of the foothills. This is Black Lake, protected by Osha Mountain whose Pass provides a route to Taos. Originally, the land was settled by the Moache Utes and used by the Taos Pueblo for summer cattle grazing.

In the winter of 1836, a mountaineer, Albert Pike, almost froze to death while crossing Osha Pass. A Taoseño family nursed him back to health by treating his severe frostbite with a homemade remedy of boiled onions and a variety of herbs. The isolation of the Spanish-Mexicans necessitated a creative culture based on their environment. Natural medicinal cures were only one example.

These were the descendants of the Spanish Conquistador and the Mexican Indian. After the Spanish Reconquest of New Mexico in 1692, they settled in the Rio Grande valleys, developing a lifestyle combining both traditions. Pueblo culture, with its knowledge of the land for centuries, also contributed to their survival techniques. However, aggressive Comanche and Mescalero Apache tribes were a constant threat to both Spanish Mexicans and the Pueblos. The nomadic tribes often attacked the settlements, stealing cattle, and kidnapping women and children. As we shall see, one of the original settlers of Black Lake suffered this experience.

When Mexico gained its independence from Spain in 1821, little changed for the New Mexican. Their geographic isolation kept them living with 16th century technology. Formal education was not a priority because there was little use for it. Knowledge of the land and its cultivation was the most important learning experience. They had a rich knowledge of irrigation principles, farming, and animal husbandry, but little interest in or information about political events swirling around them. They established a delicate balance between private property and communal land. The common land principle was essential to the survival of their lifestyle. A carefully controlled order of farming and grazing created a society where the land was used by all, but exclusively owned by none. Only the family home and adjacent garden or orchard was considered private property. The patron, or owner of a land grant, usually followed these norms especially if the workers on the land were family relatives.

The average New Mexican was poor in material goods. The majority of his belongings were homemade, from clothing to wooden plows and adobe walls. Imported items from Chihuahua such as kitchen utensils and shoes were precious commodities. Metal objects for the home or field were handed down through family generations. The barter system was the economic principle for exchange. Social life was centered around religious celebrations, baptisms, and marriages. Each village had a patron saint. His or her feast day was a time of great celebration, relieving the tedium of everyday routine. The local priest, educated and traveled, was the source of information about the outside world. It was, in a way, a benign and splendid isolation.

In 1846, the New Mexican villager looked upon General Kearny's American conquest of the territory as another political change having little effect upon his life. This time he was wrong. But not all New Mexicans were unprepared. For 25 years, the commerce along the Santa Fe Trail provided insights into what eventually might happen. In 1844, the father of J. Francisco Chaves sent his son to be educated in St. Louis, Missouri. He gave a prophetic mandate to his son: "The heretics are going to overrun this country. Go and learn their language and come back prepared to defend our people!"

When General Kearny announced in Santa Fe that the individual rights of New Mexicans would be respected, he spoke the truth as he understood it. But it was not in his control to sort out the clash between two cultures and legal systems. Culturally, the Anglo Protestant and New Mexican Catholic traditions were at odds, with highly emotional overtones carried over from the European religious wars.

Legally, the American understanding of property rights had no counterpart in the Mexican communal land concept. American law required mathematical surveys accompanied by individual or corporate title. Each New Mexican land grant, the most desired property in the territory, came under investigation. Titles had to be traced to their year of origin, sometimes going back to the early 1700s.

The Spanish Mexican method of determining boundaries by visual landmarks often produced conflicting opinions. Clever Anglo attorneys had a field day litigating clouded titles or unclear boundaries. It was not enough for the New Mexican villager to say his family had worked the land for generations. Where was his title? What part of communal land did he own? These were concepts totally foreign to the villager's thinking. He had no idea why such questions should be important. Yet the answers became clear when he was presented with painful choices. His communal land became public property, sold to the highest bidder. His financial ability to buy the land, pay taxes, or even lease the property was minimal. The person who coveted the land, and had the funds to bid for it, could destroy his patrimony. The delicate agrarian balance maintained for 150 years of Spanish Mexican rule was now in shambles.

In 1862, the United States Congress passed the Homestead Act. A citizen, or anyone intending citizenship, being 21 years or older, intending to live on the property for five years, could register 160 acres of public land for settlement. During this time, improvements were to be made. The applicant received a title which permitted him to obtain a mortgage to help pay for the improvements. There was a provision that after six months of residence, the homesteader could purchase the acreage from the government. This provision was designed to give the applicant clear title as soon as possible, rather than having to wait five years. After that, he could do whatever he wanted with the property. It appeared to be an advantageous arrangement for both parties, but it was a provision susceptible to abuse.

Black Lake, originally called Osha, was public property available for homesteading. The name Osha refers to a local plant known in English as "lovage." The stem tastes like celery, while the root can be used for medicinal purposes. The plant was known to Antonio Severino Martinez. He and his wife, Maria del Carmel (Santistevan) moved to Taos from Abiquiu in 1804 when their eldest son, Antonio Jose, was eleven years old.

Severino Martinez and his wife Guadalupe (Mares), pioneer settlers of Black Lake. (Photo courtesy of Ben Martinez)

Antonio Jose would become the most famous member of the family. After the death of his young wife, he became a Catholic priest, excelling as an educator and social activist until his death in 1867. In 1847, his brother Pascual and nephew Nestor began using the Black Lake area for the summer grazing of the family's cattle, sheep, and horses. This remained a seasonal family venture until the late 1870s. It was at this time that Severino Martinez, grandson of family patriarch Antonio Severino, took note of ominous events northeast of Black Lake, events which could jeopardize the family's 30-year use of their Osha Mountain grazing area. Severino's foresight is an example of the New Mexican becoming more discerning of land problems associated with American law.

In 1876, an ambitious and discredited politician, Steven W. Dorsey, came to New Mexico to recoup his fortune and reputation. He migrated from Kansas, where as U.S. Senator, he secured lucrative mail contracts for his transportation business. His company overcharged and underperformed its government obligations, and he was accused and convicted of fraud. Now trying to rehabilitate himself in a new venue, he brought his penchant for scheming to New Mexico.

Dorsey found a land grant, known as Una de Gato, for sale in the northeastern part of the state. He built a large two-story home, now known as the Dorsey Mansion, twenty-five miles east of present-day Springer. Then he discovered that he himself was the victim of a fraud.

Una de Gato was a bogus land grant. Dorsey devised a plan to recoup his investment and legally secure ownership of the land he thought he owned.

The solution to his problem was to use the Homestead Act in a way it was not intended. He assembled a group of individuals who applied for 160-acre parcels on the Una de Gato property, making sure that all parcels with an abundance of water were included. After filing and title were granted, Dorsey waited six months for the purchase clause of the Homestead Act to come into play. He gave the individual applicants money for the purchase price and then had each person deed their homestead acreage to him. The New Mexicans who were using the land for grazing purposes, thinking it was public land, were forcibly removed by gunfire. Dorsey had successfully manipulated the spirit of the Homestead Act.

Severino Martinez became aware of these events and saw a parallel possibility happening in Black Lake. He decided to use the Homestead Act for the purpose it was intended. He gathered a group of Taos ranchers, encouraging them to apply for Black Lake homestead parcels. He and his wife Guadalupe (Mares) intended to do the same.

It was a serious decision to move to this wilderness country, leaving the comforts of Taos where the family had roots since 1804. Severino sweetened his proposal to the other ranchers, offering to purchase their parcels if they found the land inhospitable or unprofitable. Among those agreeing to the proposal was Jose Maria Mares and his wife Jenara (Trujillo). Twenty years before, Jose had been captured by Indians, taken to Taos, and

The Severino Martinez home as it appeared in 1898. The house has been recently occupied by Robert Cook, a cousin of the Martinez family.
(Photo courtesy of Ben Martinez)

sold to Juan Mares, who adopted the boy, raising him as his own child. Such were the vicissitudes of New Mexican life in that unstable era.

Marion Shuter, a modern-day Black Lake resident, conducted research, hoping to determine from county records and U.S. patents who was the first non-Native American settler in that area. She thought at first it would be a simple procedure. She discovered that Black Lake was under the jurisdiction of Taos County until 1860, Mora County until 1869, and Colfax County from that date to the present. Records were incomplete. She found that the first survey of Black Lake was taken in 1881 by order of the Surveyor General's Office, showing two cabins to exist. No names were mentioned in the report.

A 1901 edition of the newspaper *El Nuevo Mexicano* states that Severino Martinez built the first home "around the year 1880." Robert Julyan in his book *The Place Names of New Mexico* says the first settlers were Jose and Jenara Mares. County records and U.S. patents are unclear. The earliest extant U.S. patent issued for land in Black Lake is dated February 10, 1885, some five years after actual settlement began. What is known is that by 1907 Severino Martinez owned eight claims of 160 acres each. At the time of his death in 1929, he owned most of the property in Black Lake.

The census of 1900 states that the population of Black Lake was 216. Forty-six residences were recorded. Only two heads of families were not involved in ranching or farming: Jose Sanchez who was postmaster and Antonio Ribera who was a dry-goods merchant. Postal service records state that a post office was established as Osha in 1894, changed to Blake Lake in 1903, and remained active until 1927. During the 1920s, Rafael Martinez, son of Severino, was postmaster. After 1927, Ocate, fifteen miles east of Black Lake, became the post office serving the community. Mail was delivered three times a week.

By 1910, the population dropped slightly but remained stable. Despite small numbers, three religious traditions existed in the community. The majority were Catholic, with St. Anthony's Church the center of worship. There was no resident priest. Every month a priest from Taos would come to conduct services. The 1910 census reveals the presence of a full time Methodist minister, Rev. Agapito Mares. In the 1930s, a Presbyterian church was built by sawmill owner and resident, Leandro Wheaton. It was staffed by Rev. Rubel Lucero. The church building eventually was sold and became a bar.

During these early decades, elementary schooling, consisting of grades 1-8, was well established. Two school buildings, called upper and lower, were located near present Highway 434. The 1920 census reports two teachers were employed: Jose Vigil and Eloisa Tafoya. They would be succeeded by Amelia M. Galway and Vasti Martinez. The closest high school was in Taos. When children reached high school age some families moved to Taos. Others sent their children to live with relatives during the school year.

Insights into daily life during this time are recalled by Ben Martinez. He was born in Black Lake May 1, 1917, son of Luis Martinez and Drucilla Romero. Severino was his grandfather and Padre Martinez of Taos his great-uncle. Ben lived in Black Lake until 1953, moving with his wife to Albuquerque where they still had a home into the 1990s. He recalls that for a family to survive in the years he was here, they had to be self-sufficient. Besides cattle and sheep, wheat, barley, oats, and potatoes were farming staples. They obtained beans from their Aunt Dorotea who lived in Roy, New Mexico. They exchanged their products in Mora for corn, flour, and lard. The growing season was short, winter lasting six months. People were poor but everyone had enough to eat. Ben remembers that prior to 1930, all the residents of Black Lake were Spanish Mexican except Jack Bennet and Charles Weber, who owned a ranch and also did some gold prospecting around Elizabethtown.

Ben attended the upper and lower schools. His aunts were the teachers. He rode his horse to school always in the winter months. The big event of the school year was the Christmas play. Ben's father had one of the few cars in the valley, a Model T Ford. He recalled his excitement when Palo Flechado Pass was improved for autos in the mid-1920s. It was a 1000-foot climb from the valley floor to the summit. In those days, gas flow to the engine was maintained by gravity. Fuel pumps were a thing of the future. The car would regularly stall while negotiating the upward slope. His father solved the problem by driving the car up the hill in reverse until he reached the summit.

During the Depression years, five sawmills in the valley provided work. Besides Leandro Wheaton's sawmill in Black Lake, the Continental Tie and Lumber Company operated a mill where the maintenance building of the Angel Fire Golf Course now stands, plus another sawmill at the base of Palo Flechado Pass. The CS Ranch leased grazing land and built a house for the cowboys. Everyone called the house La Casa de los Vaqueros. Ben Martinez would pass the house on his way to Agua Fria, where a general store and gas pump were located at the blinking light junction of Highways 64 and 434. A family by the name of Riley owned the Agua Fria store. This was also the bus stop to Taos and the opportunity to buy supplies like household staples and medicine. Sometimes it also involved a trip to see the doctor, Paul T. Martin, the famous "Doc" Martin of Taos. Ben was 18 when the legendary figure died. At 80 years old, Ben recalled with great pride his family heritage, especially his grandfather's service as a state legislator during the territorial days.

In 1993, a family reunion was held at Coyote Creek Park near Black Lake, 250 family members participated. The main reason for the reunion was to celebrate the 100th birthday of Drucilla Martinez, Ben's mother. Another reunion was being planned for 1998, this time in Taos.

Black Lake has maintained its quiet rural traditions. However, in

May 1988, Lear jets arrived at the Angel Fire Airport and the occupants focused on one destination: Black Lake. CBS television had chosen the lake, meadow, and Osha Mountain to be the "Montana segment" for the filming of Larry McMurtry's *Lonesome Dove*, a $15 million, twelve-hour TV mini-series to air that fall. Major stars and their support crew of 140 rented the location from Joe Torres and his UU Bar Ranch for a week.

The May 5th edition of the *Sangre de Cristo Chronicle* noted that between $30-50,000 a day would feed into the local economy. Some local residents were employed as extras. It wasn't hard to find authentic cowboy types in the Moreno Valley or Black Lake.

Since its release and many re-runs, *Lonesome Dove* has been acclaimed as a Western classic. Recently, one of the stars, Robert Duvall, was asked, what in the course of his distinguished career was his favorite role. He replied, without hesitation, his part in *Lonesome Dove*. Black Lake has achieved a certain degree of cinematic immortality.

One of the charms of New Mexico is the time-capsule appearance of its smaller communities. The changes that have taken place have not erased an era. The continuity of past and present maintains an authentic historical bond. The campsites of the Moache Utes can still be visualized. Albert Pike's ordeal through Osha Pass can still be traced. Pascual and Nestor Martinez's sheep, cattle and horses can still be imagined grazing along the banks of Laguna Negra.

Moreno Valley School Students Reminisce about the original school located between Eagle Nest and Agua Fria

Ellen Miller-Goins
Sangre De Cristo Chronicle staff writer
reprinted with permission

An Introduction to Moreno Valley Old Timers:

Elliot Andreoli has lived in the Moreno Valley 82 years (as of the year 1999). His parents, Pete and Angelina Andreoli moved to the Moreno Valley from Dawson, a coal mining community near Cimarron, when he was a baby. He attended the Moreno Valley School from 1922 to 1935. His brother, Valley resident Sam Andreoli, who is two years younger, also attended as did their other eight siblings.

Life-long Moreno Valley resident **Leo Arko, Jr.** was born to Leo and Mary Arko in 1923. Leo attended the school from about 1929 to 1938. When he graduated from 8th grade, he quit and worked on the farm until he joined the U.S. Army in 1941. He returned to the Moreno Valley in 1952.

Johnny Brandenburg, the son of Jack and Lottie Brandenburg, lived in Red River all his life. He went 1st through 6th grades in Raton, 7th and 8th grade at the Little Red School House in Red River, 9th grade in Costilla, and 10th and 11th grade at the Moreno Valley School from 1937-39. He graduated in Raton.

The parents of **Billie Burk Wilkins-Jack**, Logan and Maggie Burk, first came to the Moreno Valley in 1921 and divided their time between the Valley and a home in Mt. Dora, NM. They moved to the Valley full-time in 1934, and Billie has lived here ever since. She attended the Moreno Valley School first through 12th grades from 1935 to 1944.

Joe Gherardini moved to the Moreno Valley with his parents,

Alphonso and Frances Gherardini from Dawson in 1932 and started school here as a 10th grader that year. "I had a big class at five," Joe says.

The youngest member of the group, **Richard Johnson**, moved to the Moreno Valley from Red River in 1951. After four years of college and 22 years in the Air Force, he returned to the Valley in 1992. "Judy Swanson Piper and I were in the last class that started there in 1951," Johnson says, adding the school year was cut short by the fire.

Philip Mutz is the grandson of Herman Mutz who came to Elizabethtown in 1881. Mutz was born to Adolph and Marguerite Mutz in 1923 and lived in the Moreno Valley until the late '40s. He still has a working cattle ranch in the Valley and divides his time between Santa Fe and Eagle Nest. He attended school through the sixth grade in E'town and then the Moreno Valley School 7th through 12th grade, 1934 to 1940.

The family of **Bob Prunty** moved to the Sunshine Valley outside Questa in 1920. He was born in 1921 to C.H. and Ethel Prunty, and they moved to the Moly Mine Camp in 1923 and then to Red River in 1928 or '29. He went to school at the mine and two years at the Little Red School House. He attended the Moreno Valley School one year in 1937-38.

Ernest Swanson was born in the Moreno Valley to Ernest A. and Ada Marie Swanson in April 1917. He attended the school from 1923 to 1935. Swanson still has his ranch in the Moreno Valley and divides his time between living in the Valley and in Cimarron. "The wintertime I live in Cimarron," Swanson says. "I run cattle on my place in the summertime."

Louise Swanson McBride, Ernest Swanson's sister, was born in the Moreno Valley in 1913 and went to school from 1920 to 1932. She has lived in Cimarron for about 26 years.

Yes, They Trudged Through Deep Snow To The Old Moreno Valley School!

Everyone has heard the cliché, "When I was a kid, I had to walk five miles through four feet of snow to get to school," but in the case of some Moreno Valley residents, it was quite often true!

School days in the 1920s, '30s, and even the '40s were definitely rougher for the old-timers who attended the Moreno Valley Consolidated School, located about 6 miles south of Eagle Nest on U.S. 64 on the west side of the road. (There was a little bait shop nearby where Bob Rollins lived.) The school is only a memory now. It burned to the ground in the fall of 1952.

Six former pupils — Elliot Andreoli, Leo Arko, Jr., Billie Burk Wilkins-Jack, Richard Johnson, Ernest Swanson, and Louise Swanson McBride— along with their spouses Gina Andreoli, Lorene Arko, and Janet Arko Johnson, met at Leo Arko's mid-Valley home Tuesday, February 23, 1999, to reminisce about the Moreno Valley School.

Moreno Valley old timers met Tuesday, Feb. 23, to reminisce about the Moreno Valley Consolidated School. Left to right: Janet Arko Johnson, Louise McBride, Ernest Swanson, Richard Johnson, Elliot and Gina Andreoli and Leo and Lorene Arko. (*Chronicle* photo by Ellen Miller-Goins)

The *Chronicle* also interviewed Red River residents Bob Prunty and Johnny Brandenburg, as well as Moreno Valley rancher Philip Mutz, and long-time resident Joe Gherardini about their memories of the old school.

School History

Ernest Swanson remembers when there was a one-room schoolhouse at the same location before the larger building was built around 1928.

The school was built from logs and rock by parents and members of the community, and Joe Gherardini says it "probably had three or four rooms, plus a little matchbox gym which we played basketball in."

The school also had a kitchen and, according to its former students, the building burned in 1952 when some girls were baking pies. The old timers believe a chimney fire was the cause. Since it was the first day of elk-hunting season, all the men were hunting, so there was no one to help extinguish the blaze.

'Good morning to you ...'

The Moreno Valley group says they started every school day with the Pledge of Allegiance and the song, "Good Morning Dear Teacher."

Billie: "I can still remember the opening song" though it's been over 60 years since she attended elementary school: *"Good morning to you, good morning to you. We're all in our places with sunshiny faces ..."*

Louise Swanson: "We had a Pledge of Allegiance and then we had a prayer, but we had a teacher by the name of Jones and we'd sing 'Old Black Joe,' only we'd say Jones. We didn't like Jones."

Joe Gherardini said the school's curriculum stressed the basics: "Arithmetic, literature, history, algebra, typing and a smidgen of geometry."

A 1938-39 yearbook belonging to Johnny Brandenburg states, "Moreno Valley School offers Vocational, Commercial and College Preparatory courses. The vocational offerings consist of agriculture for

The Moreno Valley School in 1938

the boys and home economics for the girls. The commercial department offers bookkeeping, typing and shorthand."

Courses consisted of "three units of science, four units of English, two units of mathematics, two units of Spanish, and four units of social science … Practically every student is in one of the glee clubs and several are taking piano lessons. The percentage of students taking part in athletics and dramatics is especially high …"

Philip Mutz: "We didn't have a lot of resources. We didn't have a lot of advanced math, trigonometry, or geometry, but we got a fairly good education out of it. We had a good school with lots of extra-curricular activities, basketball, intramural, glee club, and school plays …"

Billie: "They even used to lock up the whole school and take us to Raton once a year to see a movie and buy a Coke in the drug store soda fountain."

Elliot: "Every Christmas we had a Christmas program, and the means of transportation was a sled. Your dad would hook up the team and then pick up everybody and you'd get in the open sled. If your feet got cold, all you'd do is jump out and hang on and run behind the sled to warm your feet."

The Basketball Team

Their basketball team, the Polar Bears, car-pooled to games from Raton to Ojo Caliente and everywhere in between. They took fourth in the district one year. The team was always small, so nearly everyone got drafted.

Ernest: "I wasn't much for playing basketball. I didn't like it. I still don't like it. I played, but not very good. The two Andreoli boys were the basketball players."

Joe: "There was no seating. You had to stand on the sidelines to watch those guys play basketball."

Johnny: "The ceilings were lower so to make a long shot, you had to be pretty good. Anytime we had visitors, we'd always win. Their ball would hit the ceiling! The visitors were used to making high, long shots, and it wouldn't work.

"Tal 'Junior' Neal could take a ball down the court faster than anyone I've ever seen."

Winter protection: legs wrapped in gunny sacks!

Leo remembers walking "about a mile and a half" to get to school, but harsh winter weather made the trip a little more arduous. During a storm, sometimes the only way they could find their way home was by following the fence line.

Louise: "That's right. We did, the Andreolis and the Swansons. We'd grab one another's coat tails, and the leader would lead us up along the fence. That's what our parents told us to do."

Gina: "When they were walking to school, they used to have to wrap their legs with gunny sacks because in those days they didn't have overshoes like they have nowadays to keep warm."

Leo: "They had overshoes, but we couldn't afford to buy 'em."

Louise: "My father had a way of fixing the gunny sacks. He'd bring the corner up, then he'd wrap around on each side, then he'd tie it with a binder twine, and we had to get those back on before we'd come home."

Gina: "It looks to me like the gunny sacks would have absorbed the snow and got wet and made your feet colder."

Louise: "I know, but they kind of froze on your feet."

Elliot: "My feet didn't get cold at all."

A hearse for a school bus

According to the group, their first school bus was a dark blue hearse with no heat or seats. They rode to school by squatting down in the back, but Elliot says, "That beat walking all the way." Their second bus was a truck with benches and a handmade cab over the back.

Billie: "The first school bus, Henry Bell drove it, and he had a partition down through the center. The boys had to sit on one side and the girls had to sit on the other side."

Johnny: "Emil and Maggie Mutz had the contract to take kids from E'town to the Moreno Valley School. I was a junior in high school, and I drove the 'bus' which was an International pickup they used during the school year as a bus and during the summertime as a pickup.

"All the boys wanted to ride on my bus 'cause they were all smoking. All the girls rode John Haddow's bus.

"One year a blizzard was coming in, so Creecy (Carson Creecy, the school principal) dismissed school at 2 o'clock. We didn't get to Eagle Nest until 6 o'clock. It was about 5-1/2 or 6 miles. All traffic was stopped, but we kept going.

"When we hit those drifts, I'd back up and all the boys would get out, and I'd gun it to make new tracks. They would all get behind the bus and push it. We got to Eagle Nest an hour before the big bus. They were handicapped—they didn't have any boys to push the big bus.

"We had to stay in Tal Neal's cabins in Eagle Nest. There were six boys in our cabin, and that night Tony Jr. (the son of Tony and Tillie Simion of Red River) and I stole a couple of blankets off the top. We woke up later and they were all kneeling on their beds to keep warm. T.D. Neal's cabins were not insulated."

Clearing the road

There was a gravel road in the Valley back then, with plenty of dips.

Philip: "Sometimes when the weather got snowy, we'd miss a day or two, but they did a fairly reasonable job of keeping the roads open. The roadway had a lot of dips in it, and they'd fill up with snow or in the spring they would sometimes get impassable because of the mud."

Joe: "At that time they didn't have the road machinery to handle the snow like they do today. There were times when the roads were blocked for a week at a time, and we didn't go to school. I was maybe a little disappointed—there wasn't anything to do.

"We had big snows the latter part of fall and big storms in January and February. It's all settled down now. It doesn't snow that much anymore."

Ernest: "My brother Harold worked on the highway when they hired men to shovel snow for 50 cents an hour!"

Red River Students boarded in Moreno Valley

Brandenburg and Prunty say going back and forth to Red River would have been too much of a challenge, so they found places to stay in the Moreno Valley during the school year.

Johnny: "Tony Jr. and I lived with the Mutz's in the bunkhouse at the ranch during the school term. The cabin we lived in had cracks in the walls, so we kept a tarpaulin on our bed to keep the snow off our bedding."

Bob: "I stayed at the T.D. Neal Camp (in Eagle Nest) in one of the cabins. I'd come home sometimes on the weekends. Once in a great while Mom would come over and stay with me for a week. I had to do my homework there by kerosene lamp."

Work and school

The Moreno Valley used to be more of a farming community with area residents growing cabbage, lettuce, peas, carrots, onions and potatoes.

Leo: "When we went to school they used to serve us onion soup …"

Louise: "Or potato soup. You know I don't care for potato soup to this day. It didn't have any seasoning in it. It was just milk and potatoes."

Philip: "A lot of the older male students worked at home, especially in the fall of the year. The Moreno Valley was agricultural at the time, and in the fall of the year when we had to move the cattle around, we'd miss school for a few days."

Elliot: "We used to take off to pick potatoes. We'd get one sack for every ten sacks we picked. That was our pay."

Leo Arko remembers getting up at 5:30 or 6 a.m. to milk cows and do chores before they walked to school.

Louise: "Well, I milked cows and we used to set our cream cans down along the highway. A truck would come along and pick it up, and it was shipped to Trinidad, Colorado, to Jacobson Creamery."

In later years the mailman picked up the cream.

A tight-knit group

Philip called the students of the Moreno Valley School a "fairly tight-knit group" (there were seven in his graduating class), and the rest of the former students definitely agreed.

Billie: "Leo was always very protective of the younger children. They didn't pick on me too much because I'd run to Leo."

Gina: "They all had nicknames. Elliot had the nickname "Boots.""

Louise: "I think Leo had the nickname 'Poldo,' short for Leopoldo."

Bob: "I remember Helen Blades. She was a tall, slender gal, and we guys got to calling her 'High Pockets.' They mostly called me 'Curly' 'cause of my curly hair, or 'Curly Bob.'"

Leo: "We used to call Tony Jr. 'Rubberneck.'"

Billie: "I can remember that because he would go around and stretch his head like a turkey."

A whacking at school, a whacking at home …

As the Moreno Valley old-timers say, corporal punishment was common at their school, or as someone said during the group interview, "In those days if you got a whacking at school, you got a whacking at home too. That way the kids behaved themselves pretty good."

Elliot: "They had a paddle."

Louise: "And they used it."

Richard: "At my house, if it was minor serious, we got two shots at it; and if it was real serious, then you got three shots (from the school, mom and then dad). So, you got three shots to get it indelibly implanted in your mind that you didn't want to do that again. That was the tier system of punishment."

Playing hooky

Elliot: "On April Fool's Day the whole school played hooky. We just all got to school and decided: Well, we'll leave. Everybody took off; but one girl, Maggie Vuicich, she stayed home. She was afraid to go …"

Elliot says they all hid near the Arko's house. "Then, when it was time to catch the bus, we all went back to school and the principal called us all in the room there and said, 'Everyone that went on the hike today, we going to give you failing grades for one month … And I'll get a note to your parents, let them know what went on …'"

"He talked and talked and talked and kept watching us, and just before it was time for school to be dismissed, he says 'Well, you had an April Fool's trick today, but I had a bigger one. April Fool's!'"

More mischief

Billie: "One Halloween they took a wagon apart and put it back together on Pat Gallagher's house (he was school janitor). That was about the meanest thing that was done then, but Pat was good natured.

Everybody loved Pat."

Billie says that she also remembers an encounter with the game warden.

"We had caught a bunch of fish and were coming back over to the school. We were going to give them to the teacher, and she was going to cook 'em. We saw Tommy Holder, the game warden, coming so we crammed them down prairie dog holes. And after he went on, we went back to get them out of the prairie dog holes."

Escaping the game warden was quite a feat since Ernest remembers that Game Warden Holder "arrested his own father."

They even admit to one bout of cheating!...

Elliot: "A bunch of us got together and we just all walked down to the school and found one of the windows open and got in there and got the answers to the test we were supposed to have the next day. And, so the next day, we gave it to everybody but Maggie Vuicich. We gave all the class the answers, but everybody was supposed to miss at least one, and we weren't supposed to miss the same question.

"We took the test and after the results were in, the teacher said, 'I can't believe this. Everybody made a better grade than Maggie did!'"

... And to smoking in the school yard!

Johnny Brandenburg says all the boys took blacksmithing "so we could sneak outside and have a smoke."

School days in the old Moreno Valley Consolidated School were pretty tame by today's standards.

Moreno Valley Life, As Remembered

The Swanson Family Settles in the Moreno Valley

by Judy Swanson Piper

My great-grandparents, Albert and Amelia Swanson, came to the United States from Sweden in 1887. They arrived in La Junta, Colorado, where Albert worked doing farming until his death in 1894. They came into the US by way of Ellis Island, but she became a naturalized citizen in 1901.

After Albert's death, Amelia remarried and again her husband passed away, in a mining accident. She moved to Cimarron, New Mexico, in 1909 where she ran a boarding house. In 1910, she moved to Elizabethtown where she established a boarding house for the gold miners. When she felt she could no longer run her boarding house, they numbered the logs of her cabin and moved her and her cabin to her son's ranch at the foot of

Original Swanson Home

Jackson Hill. She lived in that cabin until her death in 1927 of influenza.

Amelia's boarding house was on the hill above the Mutz Hotel/Saloon.

Ernest Swanson, Amelia's son, came from Sweden before the turn of the century. He worked his way over to the United States from Sweden three times on steamships, by shoveling coal into the boiler. Like his parents, he settled in La Junta. He sent for Ada Fardig Olson to come from Sweden and they were married in La Junta where he worked as a fireman for the Pacific Railroad.

They had a daughter Sigrid and a daughter Ingrid, who drowned accidently in an irrigation ditch, and a son Harold before they moved to Moreno Valley. We have the receipt for $75 that was paid as a down payment on the ranch purchased from Thomas Jackson, whose name is still used to designate Jackson Hill. The ranch purchased was 610 acres and a building was moved from Black Lake since there was no house on the place,. One story was that it was a sheepherder's shack and another is that it was a dance hall. Knowing the history of Black Lake, it might have been both at one time or another.

Great Grandma Amelia with all her grandkids near the boarding house.
(Ernest is the smallest boy standing by Great Grandma's lap)

Swanson Family
Grandma Ada holding Ernest, Louise, Grandpa Ernest, Harold, Sigrid

Grandpa "Andy" farmed wheat, oats, barley and raised timothy and clover hay for their Brown Swiss milk cows. Ada used the cream from the cows to wax the wood floors in the house, and Louise and Ernest Alfred were born to the couple in the little house. They added a living room and another bedroom to one side of the rectangular building. Dad remembers they had a housewarming and the neighbors helped celebrate. He also remembers that Amelia's wake was held in the living room.

The 50 head of milk cows were milked by my dad, his brother Harold and a neighbor, Guido Andreoli. They produced enough milk to sell throughout the Moreno Valley and some that they shipped to Trinidad in large milk cans. Grandpa also sold beef to the people who lived in Baldy Town. The road to Baldy Town was very steep and they had to back up the road so that the car would run because this was before fuel injection pumps that allowed gas powered vehicles to go uphill.

Joined by A. J. Sargeant, Mathias Heck and Charles Gallagher, a cooperatively operated cheese factory was established on the Heck ranch (known as the Monte Verde Ranch) across the road from Grandma

Amelia's cabin on the Swanson Ranch. The cheese factory building was built of stone by a man from Maxwell, and an Italian man made the cheese. Cheese sold for $2.30 per hoop.

Cheese Factory

Cheese Factory in background
Grandpa Ernest holding granddaughter Judy (Swanson) Piper

The Swansons sold crops of potatoes, lettuce, and carrots commercially for several years. One year they had a crop of 2000 bags. My dad was 12 when his mother Ada passed away in 1932. She died of Sugar Diabetes before they had the shots to help diabetics. Dad and Grandpa were "batching," and they had to decide whether to build a new house or a barn. The barn won out. All the wood came from the Moreno Valley Ranch, and the tin for the roof was ordered from Montgomery Wards and shipped by train to Ute Park and freighted from there to the ranch. Clyde Howe was one person who helped in building the barn. The barn was finished in 1937. The barn housed pigs (pork sold for 8 cents per pound), cattle (sold at 7 cents per pound), horses and hay. The potatoes were sold at 10 cents a pound.

Swanson Barn built in 1937

There was a bunk house at one time, and it housed the Taos Indians who helped with the farming. Dad said the Indians would bathe in the Hewitt Creek, and it runs cold. Grandma Ada made butter and sold some to T.D. Neal's store at 30 cents a pound.

In 1932 a family with no income that needed work was allowed to live in the bunk house, and Grandpa Andy bought shoes for the kids because they had none. This family helped build the root cellar that we still used until 2020 when a portion of the roof fell in. It previously stored vegetables and canned goods that we prepared in good years.

Dad and his siblings, Louise, Sigrid and Harold, recall walking or skiing on homemade skis to school at the regional school located on the

Dabovich place before the log schoolhouse was built. Students came from Red River, Elizabethtown, Therma (now called Eagle Nest), and Black Lake to attend the log school. They went through high school together from the 1930s to 1952 when the building burned down. The families of the Moreno Valley built the log school out of local logs, and it was a great facility. It had not only an elementary and high school, but also a gymnasium and a stage. When they replaced the floor of the stage, Dad purchased the old boards and replaced the floor in the dining room of the Swanson house.

Moreno Valley School, ca. 1938

Snow was plentiful back then, and many times school was out for a month at a time because of bad weather. Louise tells about climbing up a ladder to a hole at the top of the door of the house and sliding out to go to school. I'm sure life was hard with that much snow to contend with.

For pleasure, there were dances and silent movies at the schoolhouse or time spent listening to Grandpa Andy play his guitar with local musicians. There were also card games, ice skating and gambling in Eagle Nest in the 1930s.

Grandpa Andy owned stock in the Moreno Valley Telephone Company established in the 1920s by T.D. Neal. The company failed, but it did bring a single telephone line up the Cimarron Canyon to the T.D. Neal Mercantile building in Therma and down the Valley to Aqua Fria. This line provided telephone service for many Moreno Valley homes and businesses. In addition to being one of the first phone company stockholders, Andy Swanson was an original board member of the Eagle

Electric Cooperative that began in 1939. It became known as the Kit Carson Electric Cooperative in 1943.

My mother, Mary (McNutt) Swanson, moved with her parents and sister Ruth to New Mexico from Kentucky after her mother, Elizabeth McNutt, contracted Tuberculosis. Another sister, Cloutine, burned to death when her nightgown caught on fire and Grandma Elizabeth couldn't get the fire put out. My Grandpa, Rollie McNutt, was a Methodist preacher in Mills, Springer, and Cimarron. Mom graduated from Cimarron High School in 1933 and went to college at UNM. She taught school on the French Tract between Cimarron and Springer during the dust bowl days. She also taught school in Eagle Nest and Cimarron for many years. She married Ernest Swanson in 1940.

I understand that the first time Dad asked Mom out, she turned him down, so he decided he would never ask her again. The neighbor boys, Elliott and Sam Andreoli, plotted against him and invited Mom to go to a ballgame in Taos with them. They knew Dad would be going to play ball, so they were forced together and, as they say, the rest is history.

Dad enlisted in the Army Air Corps after his friend Guido was killed in WWII. Mom followed Dad to Big Spring, TX, where he was stationed in 1942. She taught school there as well.

After the war, Dad worked at all kinds of jobs. Grandpa Andy asked the other siblings to sign the ranch over to Dad because Dad stayed to help with the farm. The milk cows were sold, and Dad ran beef cattle because he did not like to milk cows. On the other hand, Harold liked to milk cows so well that he worked at dairies all his life, including in Ojo Caliente, Taos, and Arizona.

Dad also raised hay which he used to feed the cattle and sold to others. He sold the best hay to Charles Springer who ran racehorses. When there was plenty of water to irrigate, there was plenty of hay. I helped put more than 5000 bales in the hayloft of the barn. When it was dry, there was very little hay.

When I was growing up, the post office was in the T.D. Neal Mercantile in Eagle Nest. One side was a grocery store, and there was a small room that housed the postmaster, Annie Haddow. She was the postmaster for many years. There was also a garage next door to the grocery store. I don't know what happened to it. There were lots of bars. The Laguna Vista is one of the survivors. There was one run by Paul Yaksich, and I don't remember the name, but I remember playing in the back room while the parents were enjoying themselves in the bar.

There was open gambling in the 1930s, and Dad remembers gambling with Long John Dunn at the Laguna Vista when Gene and Pearl Wilson owned it. He also remembers Lucille Ball coming to Eagle Nest to gamble when she was filming in the area. Rumor has it that the one-armed bandits (slot machines) that the sheriff confiscated are at the bottom of Eagle Nest Lake.

Therma was very small compared to Elizabethtown. E'Town was the county seat when New Mexico was still a Territory. After Elizabethtown's demise, Colfax County seat was moved to Cimarron for a few years, then to Springer, and then to Raton. It was in the 1930s that the beautiful courthouse in Raton was built.

One of my favorite stories about Elizabethtown is the one where my Uncle Frank McBride (married to Louise) ran the sheriff out of town. The McBride family owned the ranch that was later sold to the Mutz family. Sheriff Beimer, a cousin of my dad, sent word to the three McBride brothers not to come to town that particular night. Well, this made Frank mad, so he went to town and called Sheriff Beimer out of the saloon, and proceeded to run the sheriff out of town.

My Uncle Bill Brewster, married to Sigrid, worked in the mining camp named Baldy Town. His daughter Cathryn learned to walk in Baldy Town. When she came down from Baldy Town, she found walking very different because there wasn't a slope to contend with.

Angel Fire was just a bumpy, swampy area that people passed through to get to Black Lake. In 1964, the LeBus family decided to build a ski area. They were oil people and had the money and a dream to develop a resort area. We had lots of winter snow at that time, so it was appealing.

The Moreno Valley was more-or-less comprised of dirt farmers or ranchers, but it was a community. As far away as Black Lake, we were all neighbors. We would come together at school and community functions. The thing I remember about the community was that everybody helped each other and generally got along. There were always "Hatfields and

McCoys," but for the most part everyone helped each other. I remember one year when I was in grade school, we had a masquerade ball at the schoolhouse. Everyone, even people with no kids, came dressed up. I remember Jimmy Martin, who owned the Golden Eagle at one time, came dressed up as a monkey grinder, tuxedo and all. What fun we had!

Taos was the closest town to us, but they also had lots of snow at that time, so we made many trips to Raton for groceries, etc. Mom took me to Taos for ballet lessons and piano lessons. I also belonged to the Order of Rainbow for Girls in Taos.

We raised a garden every summer and had beef, and sometimes deer, in winter. We went fishing and had trout sometimes. I remember going to the little Arko Grocery that was on County Road B-8. I can still remember seeing all the cans on the shelves and the old wooden meat counter where Mrs. Arko would reach in and get meat to slice. In the winters, everyone had to stock up on staples like flour, sugar, etc., but I remember the Watkins salesman driving up to the house to sell spices and vanilla.

There were doctors in Taos, but Mom preferred the ones in Raton, so that is where we went. We also banked in Raton.

Being good neighbors is important to me. In the "old days," neighbors would get together to help each other and volunteer to do things for the betterment of the community. That is the part I miss most because it seems not to happen that way anymore—it seems the younger generations and most of those new to the Valley are looking out just for themselves, which is very sad. The cliché "Ask not what your Country can do for you but what you can do for your Country" has long been forgotten. Since our Old Timers are dying off, who is going to step in to fill the gap? I already miss the Old Timers and their stories!

* * *

Judy Piper Swanson Piper is a 4th generation Moreno Valley descendant. Judy was raised in the Moreno Valley, attended grade school and high school in Eagle Nest and Cimarron, and graduated from Cimarron High School in 1964. Judy and her husband Burke Piper returned to the Moreno Valley to manage the Swanson Ranch that was started by her grandparents in 1910. Judy's daughter Jo and husband Mike have since joined Judy and Burke on the Swanson Ranch, and the granddaughters are frequent visitors. (Photos are from the archives of Judy Swanson Piper.)

The Bull's History in Moreno Valley
by Kay (Bull) Moore

Bruce Bull, Jr. came to the Moreno Valley with his parents, Bruce and Polly Murchason Bull, and brother Dick and sister Horton in July 1928 from Lefors, Texas. The rest of his siblings Blanche, Charlotte, Anna, Clifford, and Clinton came later to either visit or live.

They had been through the Valley a couple times and Bruce Jr.'s Dad decided he liked it here. The family sold their ranch in Texas and bought the 3500 acre Black Lake Ranch. They ran about 300 head of whiteface (Hereford) mother cows. They put up a lot of hay in the summer. They liked it in Moreno Valley—there weren't many people, and most of the ones here were ranchers and farmers. It was before anyone controlled fishing on Eagle Nest Lake, and people would fish whenever they had the time and opportunity to do so.

One of Ruth (Seargeant) Bull's favorite pastimes was growing flowers. Ruth was a native of Texas and arrived in the Moreno Valley in 1931

Most at home on his horse, Andy, Bruce Bull Jr., a Texas native, became a Moreno Valley resident in 1928

180

In 1931, Ruth arrived with her parents, A.H. and Gertrude (Chance) Seargeant, along with three of her sisters: Geneva, Evelyn, and Fay (with her husband Lem Tunstall). They all settled on a farm which is now part of Val Verde properties. Everything they brought was shipped by train to Ute Park, including mules, five or six Jersey milk cows, and the farming equipment. Ruth's father, A.H., raised potatoes, oats, and barley. During the Depression, times were very difficult. They had plenty to eat, but A.H. couldn't make a good enough living, so A.H., Gertrude, Fay and Lem returned to Borger, Texas.

Ruth stayed in the Moreno Valley and taught 1st through 5th grades at the old Moreno Valley log schoolhouse for four years until Bruce Jr. and Ruth married in 1936. After that, she was busy raising their six children—five girls, Betty, Kay, Jean, Yvonne (Toots), and Janice, and one son Bruce III (Bud).

In 1944, the Bull family sold the ranch to the McDaniel brothers. Bruce Jr.'s parents moved back to Lefors, and Bruce Jr. and his wife, Ruth (Seargeant) Bull, moved to the Siemantel Place, which is now known as the Girl Scout Camp Elliot Barker, and consisted of over 1,700 acres. Bruce, Jr. leased the Siemantel Place for several years to graze cattle.

In the late 1950s and early '60s, Bruce Jr. hauled treated poles for the LeBus brothers' pole plant at Agua Fria (now the blinking light).

In 1966, Mike Cunico asked Bruce Jr. to lease the Cunico Ranch, so Bruce Jr. leased Cunico's 700 acres and some other ranches in the Valley to graze cattle. In 1979, Bruce Jr. stopped grazing cattle and turned the operation over to his daughter and son-in-law, Kay and Leroy Moore. In 2021 Kay and Leroy Moore continue to reside in the Moreno Valley and graze cattle.

Bruce III (Bud) joined the US Air Force in the late '50s. Due to an accident in the early 1960s, he received an honorable disability discharge; and Ruth was devoted to caring for Bud until his death in 2002.

Ruth always remembered the Valley's cold weather and her first sleigh ride with Margaret Kletke. The Kletkes once owned the ranch across from the junction of Highways 64 and 434.

Bruce Jr. was an avid hunter, hunting mostly bear and mountain lion on horseback with dogs. He also led hunting trips for other hunters for several years.

Steam mill that was at Cieneguilla Creek, Black Lake & Agua Fria

The Jim Blades' Agua Fria Store with living quarters

Eagle Nest about 1940

After Bruce and Ruth retired, they moved to Arizona.

* * *

Kay Bull Moore is a 3rd generation descendant of the Moreno Valley. She is the second of Bruce Jr. and Ruth Bull's six children. Kay and her husband Leroy Moore are lifelong residents (except for a few years) of the Moreno Valley where they graze cattle. Their son, Kyle Moore, his wife Cindy, and their two grandchildren also live in the area. (Photos are from Kay Moore.)

Jim Blades Sawmills in Moreno Valley

by Jimmy Blades

In 1937, Jim Blades was living in Lequire, Oklahoma, where he had a sawmill. The lumber business was slow so he started looking around and heard about the possibility of cutting timber off the Maxwell Land Grant. Jim contacted Mr. van Lint and made the necessary arrangements to move to Moreno Valley. His family, consisting of his wife Carrie and children Jewell, Helen, Paul, Louise, Peggy; and his married son Nob and his wife Lorene, all loaded into Jim's pickup along with their household belongings and headed to New Mexico. The first place they stayed was at Arko's Cabins located about five miles south of Eagle Nest. The name of the town had been changed from Therma to Eagle Nest not long before

In picture left to right: Nob Blades, Gaines White, Paul Blades,
Jim Blades and Ellis Overstreet

they moved to Moreno Valley.

In 1938, the company Jim was working for went bankrupt. Trees were being cut on the Maxwell Land Grant owned by the Maxwell Land Grant Co. in Holland. Mr. van Lint was looking after their interests. Jim assumed the contract of the bankrupt company. The Charles Ilfield Company sold

Sawmill located on Idlewild road

him a steam mill, located on the Cieneguilla Creek off the Black Lake road. From Cieneguilla, Jim moved the mill to Black Lake because most of the logs were hauled by horse and wagon, so the mill needed to be close to where the timber was cut.

In 1940, Jim bought a place at Agua Fria, at the corner of the turn off to Black Lake. It was a store with two gas pumps and living quarters. He moved the mill behind the store. By then, trucks were hauling the logs.

The highway (US-64) through the valley was gravel and remained gravel until the 1950s. The road to Black Lake was a dirt road and remained dirt until sometime in the 1940s when it was graveled.

As the lumber was shipped out, the trucks had to stop and check with Ben Tepe. Ben Tepe owned a service station and cabins in Eagle Nest, so it was no trouble for the trucks to stop before leaving the Valley. Most of the lumber, whether regular one inch, two inch, or ties were taken to Ute Park and loaded on a train for shipment to their destination.

In 1942, Jim Blades sold the sawmill and bought a farm on the French Tract between Springer and Cimarron.

When World War II started, the Defense Department came to Jim Blades and asked if he would be interested in going back into producing lumber. They told him they would help him get the necessary equipment to return to sawmilling. Jim agreed and, after an absence of two or three years, returned to sawmilling in Moreno Valley. The first location of the mill was just outside of Eagle Nest on the Idlewild road, and it remained there for a few years. Jim's son, Paul, helped run the sawmill. His other son, Nob, built log roads and ran the logging operation in the woods (forest).

In 1949, the First National Bank of Raton came to Jim with a proposal. They had acquired the old Habager place about five miles south of Eagle Nest and offered to sell it to him. After some negotiations, Jim Blades bought the forty acres and moved the sawmill five miles south of Eagle Nest where it remained until Jim Blades sold the mill to Floyd and Cotton Ison, and Jim retired.

In the early 1950s, lumber sales were nonexistent. Jim Blades' sons,

Jim Blades sawmill at the corner of Highway 64 and County Road B-8 with Arko Cabins in the close background. The original home of Leo Arko, Sr. is immediately below forest, and the Leo Arko, Jr. home is between the original Arko, Sr. home and the Arko Cabins.

Nob and Paul, bought a truck, which they loaded with lumber, and Paul drove to Oklahoma, Arkansas, Louisiana, and Texas to sell the lumber. No one would buy the lumber, so Paul brought it back to the Moreno Valley. Although lumber was not selling, Jim's sheer willpower had the loggers continue cutting trees, hauling logs, and Jim continued operating the mill. Logs were piled high in the log yard; lumber was stacked throughout the lumber yard; but to keep the employees on the payroll, Jim kept the mill operating.

Then after one bad year, builders started building again. Lumber was shipped out daily. In a short time, all the lumber was sold. Lights were strung, and the mill was operating on two shifts—Paul running the day shift and Nob running the night shift.

In 1951, Jess Parsons made arrangements to put a planer at the sawmill. He ran it for a couple of years, then sold it to Jim.

In 1952, REA built an electric power line, and Jim converted from diesel engines to electric motors.

In 1955, Jim purchased the timber on Tolby and American Creek from Ed Springer, and Paul Blades oversaw the logging of this timber.

In 1957, Jim sold the sawmill to the Isons, and Paul Blades continued logging the timber on Tolby and American Creek.

From 1937 to the late 1950s, except for two or three years, Jim Blades was the largest employer in Moreno Valley. He had a total of about 60 employees who had jobs ranging from working in the sawmill, the planer, in the woods cutting trees, skidding the logs down the mountain, and loading the logs on trucks the haulers used to take the logs to the sawmill.

In 1951, the First Baptist Church of Springer decided to start a mission in Moreno Valley. The Church came to Jim with the proposition of putting the Church on Jim's land. Most of the young people in the Valley were the children of Jim's employees, so Jim agreed with the Church's proposal to build the mission on his land. Jim furnished the lumber to build the mission. The sawmill hands, their wives, including Jim's wife Carrie, and all the children helped to build the mission.

The Eagle Nest Baptist Mission became a part of the Cimarron Baptist Church. After Jim retired, the building was moved to Eagle Nest. In 2021 the building is still located on the property of the Eagle Nest

Baptist Church as an outbuilding.

Eagle Nest Baptist Mission on the 40 acres owned by Jim Blades in the 1950s

The Day of the Blue Snow

On May 16, 1955, we awoke to a beautiful spring day. The air was clear, there was not a cloud in the sky, and there was not even a hint of a breeze. In short, it was a perfect spring day.

The day was so beautiful I (Jimmy Blades) wore a short sleeve shirt and Indian moccasins to school. I was attending high school at Cimarron High School, about thirty miles away.

By the time we got to school, we could see a few billowy white clouds beginning to form. The clouds built up very quickly, and it began to snow.

At nine o'clock that morning, my father Nob, who worked at the Blades Lumber Mill, left to deliver a load of lumber nineteen miles away over the mountains. He had not yet arrived at the delivery site when it began to snow. The snowflakes were huge, looking like silver dollars as they drifted silently to the ground in the still air.

By the time the lumber was unloaded, the road back over the mountain was impassable. My father decided the best thing to do was to go about a hundred miles around to take the road that was not as steep and better maintained. As he went down the canyon, the snow continued to fall, getting deeper and deeper.

Meanwhile, at the school, the snow continued to get heavier and heavier. There was still no wind, so the snow was building up like a blanket. By the time school was out, there was about a foot of new snow on the ground.

The school bus was a station wagon. As we went up Cimarron Canyon to go over McAvoy Hill (a steep incline nearly a mile long) into the Moreno Valley where I lived, the snow kept getting deeper and deeper. The snow was so deep that it was above the front bumper. The station wagon was pushing the snow and the tires couldn't get enough traction to climb the steep incline. Using our feet and hands, we cleared some of the snow from in front of the station wagon. We still had to back up about three-fourths of a mile several times, to get a run up this incline.

When I got home, it was well after dark and my father still wasn't home. My mother was getting worried. After all, he had left at 9 a.m. to go nineteen miles, unload some lumber and return home.

Finally, about midnight, we heard a truck coming. My father had been fighting the snow for nearly fifteen hours and had been stuck twice. The last time he got stuck, he was nearly in sight of the house, but he was finally home.

The next morning when we got up, the snow was three feet deep on the level. The wind had not blown as the snow fell during the night and did not blow all the next day either.

The next day the sun came out bright, and the sky was clear. The snow had a barely noticeable blue tint as if the sky was reflecting off it. Naturally, there was no school that day, so we had a great time playing in the new snow. As we played in the snow, we noticed that where we stepped and looked down in the hole, the light filtering through the snow made the air in the hole blue.

On August 1, 1994, The National Atomic Energy Laboratory at Los Alamos, N.M. released a story saying that: "In Eagle Nest, in northern New Mexico, blue snow fell on May 17-18 after the 28-kiloton bomb was detonated as part of a series of tests at the Nevada Test Range."

After Jim Blades Retired

When the Isons sold the sawmill and moved, Paul and June Blades bought the 40 acres from the them and moved to the property.

R.S. Lesage, who owned the Moreno Ranch, built a sawmill named Moreno Lumber Company to process the timber cut on Moreno Ranch. Paul Blades managed the sawmill and the logging operation for Lesage. June Blades, Paul's wife, did the bookkeeping.

After Lesage sold the sawmill to Big Three Lumber in the early 1970s, Paul and June built and operated the first lumber and hardware store in the Moreno Valley, Valley Builders, in Eagle Nest. Paul and June later sold Valley Builders to George Erickson and Frank McCullough. Frank McCullough was the first Mayor of the Village of Eagle Nest in 1976 when Eagle Nest was incorporated as a Village.

* * *

Jimmy Blades is the first-born grandchild of Jim and Carrie Blades, and the first-born child of Nob and Lorene Blades. He attended school at the Moreno Valley School until it burned in 1952. He graduated from Cimarron High School in 1956. In 1957, he moved with his family to Oklahoma, and they purchased the Butcher Pen Resort on Lake Texoma. Over the years, Jimmy has researched his family history. Jimmy and his wife, Linda, currently live in Texas. (Photos are from the archives of Jimmy Blades.)

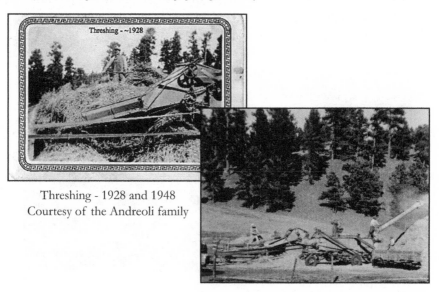

Threshing - 1928 and 1948
Courtesy of the Andreoli family

The Andreoli Family

by Lynette Andreoli Holbrook,
Linda Andreoli, Ginelle Andreoli

Pietro (Pete) Andreoli was born in Fabriano, Italy, in 1878. At the age of 19, he immigrated to the United States through Ellis Island and settled in Iron Mountain, Michigan, where he began working in the iron mines. There he met Angelina Svaizer (Italian-Austrian descent), and the couple married in 1904. In 1908, they relocated to Dawson, New Mexico, a mining community of about 5,000, and Pete continued to work as a coal miner.

After hearing about the "dark, rich soil" of the Moreno Valley, Pete and Angelina and their seven children moved to the Moreno Valley in 1917 and purchased 40 acres at $5 an acre from the Maxwell Land Grant. This was the beginning of the Andreoli Farm. Eventually more acres were added for a total of 217 acres. Work horses and early farm machinery cleared and leveled the land. Neighbors helped build the farmhouse and dig a root cellar. Soon after, the barn and other outbuildings were built. Over time, three more children were added to the family.

Angelina & Pete Andreoli - 1943

During the early years, small crops were planted and harvested by hand. Pete cut hay with a scythe and Angelina would rake it with a hand rake and put it into bundles. A horse-drawn hay wagon was used to carry the bundles to the barn for storage. As more acreage was added, additional farm machinery was purchased to plant and harvest crops of winter and summer wheat and oats. Some of this grain was kept as feed for the horses and cows. The rest was hauled to Alamosa, Colorado, to be ground into flour for family use.

Lettuce Ready to Deliver to Market - 1956

Pete Andreoli - 1940's

They grew acres of lettuce, which they sold at stores in nearby towns. Twenty-five acres of potatoes were planted in May and harvested in October. Families from the Moreno Valley and surrounding areas were invited to pick the potatoes that were later sold to a Texas company. Those who helped with the harvest were given one free sack of potatoes for every

Gina Andreoli - 1940's

191

10 sacks they picked. Potatoes were often traded for supplies at Rosso's store in Cimarron.

In addition to farming, they raised milk cows, and sold milk and cream to the Co-op Cheese Factory in the Valley and in Trinidad, Colorado. They butchered their own livestock, chickens and pigs. Meat was preserved by either smoking it in a smokehouse, covering and hanging it in the root cellar, or salting it and/or covering it with lard before storing it in crocks.

When they weren't working on the farm during harvest, the Andreoli

Moreno Valley High School Basketball Team, the "Polar Bears" - 1934
Sam & Elliot are 6th and 8th from the left

children (Bino, Johnny, Helen, Anna, Guido, Edith, Elliot, Sam, Katie, and Rosie) attended the Moreno Valley School. Winters were harsh and they had to walk a mile and a half in many feet of snow to get to the school. To keep warm, Angelina would wrap children's legs with gunny sacks. The children would take their lunch from home. Lunch consisted of "sandwiches" made with potato slices or cabbage leaves.

Farm life was hard, but Pete and Angelina found time for entertainment. Many times they loaded everyone onto the horse drawn wagon and joined other families at Saturday night dances or school programs.

As time went on and the children got older, things changed. The girls got married, and the boys were drafted into the military during WWII.

The war was very hard on the family, especially for Angelina who became a Gold Star mother when her son Guido was killed aboard a Japanese Bataan POW "Hell Ship" in October of 1944.

After serving in the military, Elliot and Sam returned to the farm to help their parents. Elliot married Gina Gherardi whose family also came from Dawson, and they had three daughters (Lynette, Linda and Ginelle). Elliot and Sam continued farming, as well as taking on other jobs. Elliot worked with the Colfax County Assessor's office in Raton, surveying farms and ranches in the area. Later both Elliot and Gina worked as school bus drivers. Sam worked with Colfax County maintaining county roads. Both Elliot and Sam took on carpentry jobs and built many cabins in the Moreno Valley, including in the Willow Creek and Lakeview Pines area. They also helped build the Country Club at the Angel Fire Golf Course and worked on the expansion of St. Mel's Catholic Church. Gina kept busy as a farm wife, raising three daughters and working in the fields. Everyone helped maintain a bountiful vegetable garden. Pete and Angelina continued to live and work on the farm for the remainder of their lives.

The year 2017 marked the 100th anniversary of the 217-acre homestead, which has since passed on to Elliot and Gina's three daughters, granddaughters of Pete and Angelina Andreoli.

* * *

Lynette Andreoli Holbrook, Linda Andreoli, and Ginelle Andreoli are the daughters of Elliot and Gina Andreoli and granddaughters of Pete and Angelina Andreoli, making them 3rd generation Moreno Valley descendants. They were raised in the Moreno Valley, attended Eagle Nest Elementary and Junior High School, and graduated from Cimarron High School. They frequently return to the Moreno Valley to enjoy the area and help maintain the homestead. (Photos are courtesy of Ginelle's husband, Mark Welsh, who scanned photos in the Andreoli archives.)

Arko Family Moreno Valley History Supplement

by Agnes Arko Gibson

There is mention of the Arko Family in various places throughout *Lure, Lore, and Legends of the Moreno Valley*. This supplement provides some additional facts not previously covered.

Leopold (Leo, Sr.) and Marija (Mary) Arko purchased land in the Moreno Valley in about 1917 to raise lettuce and potatoes to sell to the coal miners in Dawson, NM. Dawson was a "Company Town" where all real estate and businesses belonged to Phelps Dodge Corporation, owner and operator of the mine. Mary managed a Company boarding house. Leo, Sr. and some of the older family boys worked in the Dawson Coal Mine. After the Arkos acquired Moreno Valley land, Leo, Sr. and the older boys farmed the Moreno Valley land during the growing season and worked in the mine during the winter.

After completion of Eagle Nest Dam in 1918 and water accumulated, the Lake was stocked with rainbow trout and became a destination for avid fishermen and tourists. Therefore, in about 1920, Leo and Mary moved the family to the Moreno Valley full time as there was now a market in the

Leo, Sr. and Mary Arko sitting on couch in their Mid Valley Store living quarters.

Moreno Valley for the sale of produce raised on the Arko Farm.

To help meet the needs of fishermen and tourists in the Moreno Valley, the Arko family established the Mid-Valley Store, Cabins, and Dance Hall at the corner of what was then Highway 64 and County Road B-8. In addition to supplying customers with fresh Arko produce, Mid-Valley Store sold canned and boxed food, household items, and sundries they purchased from Charles Ilfield Company. The cabins were rented short-term to tourists and fishermen. The dance hall was the site of frequent Saturday night dances as well as Sunday morning church services provided by the traveling Catholic priest until St. Mel's Catholic Church was built in 1936 in what is now the Village of Eagle Nest.

When Highway 64 was realigned in the late 1940s, it no longer passed in front of the Mid-Valley Store thereby reducing public visibility and business to the store. In 1949 Jim Blades installed a sawmill on the acreage bordering the new Highway 64 & County Road B-8. The sawmill workers then became the primary customers of Mid-Valley Store and long-term tenants for the cabins and the apartments created from conversion of the dance hall to apartments.

Mid-Valley Store and Cabins served the Moreno Valley until it closed

Leo Arko, Jr. on leave from US Army in 1944 with Mary & Leo Arko, Sr.
at stairs to Mid Valley Store.

in the early 1960s, when Leo, Sr. and Mary were no longer physically able to do the work of keeping the business going. Since the business location was also Leo and Mary's home, they had no interest in selling or letting someone else run the business.

Mary Arko had thirteen children; five with her first husband, Franciscus (Frank) Novak who died of miner's consumption in 1906; and eight with Leopold Arko, Sr. Her 7th child (who was name Leopold Arko, Jr.) died in 1923, so when her 12th child was born in 1923 (after the death of her 7th child) her 12th child was named Leopold (Leo) Arko, Jr. although technically he was Leopold Arko III.

The second Leopold (Leo) Arko, Jr. lived and worked on the Arko

Leo Arko, Jr. home on leave standing in front of the farm tractor and Mid-Valley Cabins in 1944.

Farm until World War II when he joined the war effort by working as a welder for Kaiser Shipbuilding Company, building Liberty Ships at one of Kaiser's Richmond, CA shipyards. Leo then joined the Army in 1944. After training to operate Army Tanks at Ft. Hood, Texas, he was sent to Europe where he operated an Army tank until the war ended.

In 1952 Leo, Jr. returned to the Arko Farm with his wife Lorene and their three oldest children. Leo, Jr. and Lorene had seven more children who were all raised on the Arko Farm. All the children had assigned jobs, which included chores like watching the younger children, tending the chickens, picking and cartoning eggs, gardening, tending and milking cows and, when older, plowing fields and helping to harvest hay and grain in the years there was enough rain for the grain to mature.

In 1953, after a year of full-time farming, Leo, Jr. found that farming wasn't as profitable as it had been in earlier years and/or the cost of living had increased substantially. So he had to supplement the family income by working other jobs. Over the years, those jobs included working at the Blades Sawmill, hauling logs to the sawmill, building logging roads, and operating equipment to maintain State and County roads.

Leo Arko Jr. and Lorene on their 50th Wedding Anniversary

In addition to raising ten children and doing farm chores, Lorene taught religious classes at St. Mel's Catholic Church and was the cook/custodian at Eagle Nest School for many years starting in 1973. After a few years of retirement from the school, she helped keep the Eagle Nest Senior Center operating by taking on the cook/custodian position when the newly built Senior Center was on the verge of closing because a cook/custodian couldn't be found—during this time, Leo, Jr. had to oversee milking the cows in addition to his job maintaining county roads.

Lorene served in many community organizations including the Moreno Valley 4-H Club, and she participated in the Colfax County Fair for many years. In 2005 Leo, Jr. and Lorene were the Colfax County Fair and Rodeo Grand Marshals.

As of 2021, descendants of Leo, Jr. and Lorene remain in the Moreno Valley and farm some of the land purchased by Leo, Sr. and Mary in the 1900s. These descendants agree with their parents, grandparents, and great grandparents that the Moreno Valley is the best place in the whole wide world to live. Of course, some of them haven't lived elsewhere, but they've visited enough other places to know what a gem the Moreno Valley is.

* * *

Leo & Lorene Arko Grand Marshals of 2005 Colfax County Fair & Rodeo.

Agnes Arko Gibson is a 3rd generation descendant of the Moreno Valley. She is the eldest of Leo, Jr. and Lorene Arko's ten children. After graduating from Cimarron High School in 1964, she completed Draughon's Business College in Albuquerque, and held office jobs in Albuquerque and then in the California Bay Area. Agnes and her husband Scott returned to Moreno Valley in 1998. (Photos are from the Arko family archives.)

Flip to the end of the book to see more pictures!

Sonny and Thresa Johnson's Moreno Valley History
As told by Richard Johnson

Oscar Johnson and his wife (the grandparents of Howard [Sonny] Johnson) defaulted on a loan in Sweden and lost everything in the late 1800s, so they moved their family from Sweden to Ohio, and then to Two Buttes, Colorado where Sonny was born in 1916, the 7th of 8 siblings.

Thomas J. Simons and his wife, the parents of Thresa Simons Johnson, the 12th of 13 siblings, moved from Ireland to Ohio in the late 1800s. In 1899 they moved to homestead 160 acres on the Johnson Mesa east of Raton.

Sonny Johnson attended school through the 10th grade and then worked as a carpenter and gas station attendant until joining the US Army to fight in World War II. During Sonny's Army training at Fort Polk, he helped train new recruits as snipers; but when in Europe and Africa, Sonny's carpenter skills resulted in his serving as an engineer.

After military service, Sonny returned to the Raton area in 1945 and married Thresa Simons. Sonny and Thresa acquired a couple of acres in the Bitter Creek area outside of Red River, NM. Sonny built a cabin where he and Thresa lived during the birth of their three children. Sonny continued work as a carpenter, and he was instrumental in the building of many Red River area facilities, including Tall Pines Guest Ranch, Young's Ranch, and Lazy H Guest Ranch originally owned by Dudley Hickman, the father of Bill Hickman of Cimarron, and this property is now owned by Michael Martin Murphy.

In 1951, Sonny and Thresa purchased a home in Eagle Nest so their three children could attend school, as this was before the time of school bus service in the Red River area. The Johnson home was located across the street from St. Mel's Catholic Church on North Willow Creek Drive. Sonny and Thresa lived in this home until their deaths.

In the 1950s Thresa and Sonny purchased the Snack Bar Cafe from Mrs. Mertz. The Snack Bar Cafe served three daily meals, as well as coffee, beverages and snacks throughout the day, and it was the gathering place for the latest local news. When not in school, the Johnson children helped Thresa serve customers, wash dishes, take out trash, and did other chores to keep the restaurant operational and tidy.

In the 1960s the Snack Bar Cafe property was purchased by Bob and Edith Sullivan so the Laguna Vista Lodge could put its office in that location. The Sullivans relocated the cafe building to South Tomboy Drive where it was converted to a private residence. Note: The original business known as the Laguna Vista Lodge was located on Highway 64 near the turnoff for County Road B9 to the Lakeview Pines subdivision. It is said that the old Laguna Vista building burned in the late 1940s when linseed oil used to treat the building's exterior caught fire as it was being heated on a wood stove.

During the time Thresa operated the Snack Bar Cafe, for many years Sonny operated the Eagle Nest Shamrock Gas Station for Mitchell Distributors prior to serving as the Eagle Nest Postmaster for 13 years.

After retiring from employment and business endeavors, Sonny enjoyed gardening, and he raised a bounty of vegetables, many of which were given to area residents who didn't have gardens. After the Snack Bar Cafe building was sold, Thresa enjoyed homemaking and helping to care for her grandchildren.

* * *

Richard Johnson is the eldest of Sonny and Thresa Johnson's three children, and a 2nd generation Moreno Valley Descendant. After graduating from Cimarron High School in 1964, he attended Trinidad Junior College where he graduated in 1966. Richard then attended New Mexico State University and graduated in 1968, after which he returned to the Moreno Valley and worked as a carpenter with his dad. In 1969, Richard received his US Military draft notice, so he joined the US Air Force as part of its Medical Corps where he served for 22 years. Richard returned to the Moreno Valley in 1991 to help care for his ailing mother. In 1996 Richard married Janet Louise Arko who had returned to the Moreno Valley after her service in the US Navy. Janet passed from medical complications on her birthday, November 24, 1999. In 2021, Richard continues to live in Eagle Nest.

Bibliography and Listing of Interviews

Chapter One: The Moreno Valley and the Colfax County War
Publications —
Keleher, William A., *The Maxwell Land Grant,* University of New Mexico Press, Albuquerque

Parsons, Chuck, *Clay Allison,* Pioneer Book Publishers, Seagraves, Texas

Murphy, Lawrence, *Philmont,* University of New Mexico Press, Albuquerque

Westphall, Victor, *The Colfax County War,* Research Paper presented to the New Mexico Historical Society.

Chapter Three: Native Americans in the Moreno Valley
Publications —
Stanley, F., *The Jicarilla Apaches of New Mexico,* Pampa Print Shop, Pampa, Texas, 1967

Kenner, Charles L., *A History of New Mexican Plains Indian Relations,* University of Oklahoma Press, Norman, Oklahoma, 1969

Gunnerson, Dolores A., *The Jicarilla Apaches,* Northern Illinois University Press, De Kalb, Illinois, 1974
Interviews —
Stephen Zimmer, Philmont Scout Ranch, Cimarron, New Mexico
Dr. Victor Westphall

Chapter Four: Elizabethtown—New Mexico's El Dorado
Publications —
Murphy, Lawrence R., *Philmont, a History of New Mexico's Cimarron Country,* University of New Mexico Press, Albuquerque

Looney, Ralph, *Haunted Highways,* University of New Mexico Press, Albuquerque

L'Aloge, Bob, *Knights of the Sixgun,* Yucca Tree Press, Las Cruces, New Mexico

A Souvenir of the Great Elizabethtown Gold and Copper Mining District,

published in 1902 by Rev. N.J. Wright, owner, and publisher of the *New Mexican Miner*. Its purpose was to attract more investment and settlement.
Interviews —
Beni-Jo Fulton, Founder and Director of the E'Town Museum
Les Davis, President of the CS Ranch and Cattle Company

Chapter Five: Brief Glimpses at the Valley
Publications —
"Gold Rush Town," *New Mexico Magazine,* April 1958
"The History of the Idlewild Community, 1932-1982" (unpublished). The Idlewild History Committee, Maudeline Hutton, chairperson.
"The Hole in the Wall Gang," *Badman* Magazine Fall, 1972
James, Rebecca Salsbury, *Eighteen Ladies and Gentlemen, Taos, NM (*1885-1939), Taos, New Mexico,1953
"The Lowrey Sisters: Last of a Pioneer Family," *Sangre de Cristo Chronicle,* Sept. 3, 1980
New Mexico Mines and Minerals, author unknown
Pamphlet, St. Mel's Catholic Church, Eagle Nest, New Mexico, 1996
The Records of the Methodist-Episcopal Conference of Northern New Mexico, 1868-1890 Unpublished handwritten records.
A Souvenir of the Great Elizabethtown Gold and Copper Mining District, The Elizabethtown Press, 1902
"The Orneriest One of the Bunch," by Lori Gallagher, *Sangre de Cristo Chronicle,* September 3, 1980
Obituary of William C. Gallagher, *Sangre de Cristo Chronicle,* October 9, 1988
Ancestral Chart of Gallagher Family, Joe Gallagher, Houston, Texas
Birth and death dates of John Gallagher family from old family Bible, Laurelle Gallagher
Interviews —
Leo Arko, Jr., William Bratton, Mrs. Fred W. Montague, Jr., Mrs. Robert F. Munch (personal letter), Philip Mutz, Katherine Witt Potvin, Jim Evans, Betty Fleissner, Dr. Victor Westphall, Joseph C. (Jay) Gallagher, Laurelle Errington Gallagher, Jeannine Neal

Chapter Six: Eagle Nest
Publications —
Sangre de Cristo Chronicle archives
Fugate, Francis L. and Roberta B., *Roadside History of New Mexico*, Mountain Press Publishing Company, Missoula, Montana, 1989
Interviews —
Jeannine Neal, Cathy Coppy, Margaret Pobar, Joseph Pobar, Glynda McBurnette, Betty Ketchum, Les Davis, Bruce Davis, Billie Olsen, Don Borgeson, Lee Mills, Jackie Mills, Tese Burt, Thelma Coker, Paul Atzberger

Chapter Seven: The Vietnam Veterans National Memorial and Dr. Victor Westphall
Publications —
"A Long Day's Journey," *Sangre de Cristo Chronicle,* May 26, 1994
"The Mission to Reach Out to Veterans," *Sangre de Cristo Chronicle,* May 23, 1996
"Healing Reminder," *Albuquerque Journal, 1995*
"Vietnam Veterans National Memorial, A Brief History," Dr. Victor Westphall
"A Journey of Love," Dr. Victor Westphall
"DAV, Vietnam Memorial to Go Separate Ways," *Sangre de Cristo Chronicle,* September 24, 1998
"Fundraising Under Way for Memorial," *Sangre de Cristo Chronicle,* October 1, 1998
Memorial Day Ceremony Programs, 1993-1996, The DAV Vietnam Veterans National Memorial
Veterans Day Program, 1995, The DAV Vietnam Veterans National Memorial
Interview —
Dr. Victor Westphall

Chapter Eight: Fire of the Gods and Angels
Publications —
Pearson, Jim Berry, *The Red River-Twining Area, A New Mexico Mining Story,* University of New Mexico Press, Albuquerque

Murphy, Lawrence R., *Philmont,* University of New Mexico Press, Albuquerque

Murphy, Lawrence R., *Out in God's Country,* University of New Mexico Press, Albuquerque

Bullock, Alice, *Living Legends of the Santa Fe Country,* Green Mountain Press

Waters, Frank, *The Man Who Killed the Deer,* The Swallow Press, Inc.

Sangre de Cristo Chronicle, Sun Publications Inc., Drawer I, Angel Fire, New Mexico

Enchanted Summer 1996, Sun Publications, Inc., Drawer I, Angel Fire, New Mexico

The Taos News, 120 Camino de la Placita, Taos, New Mexico

Interviews and Personal Communication —

James Butts, Bets Loving, Bob Bright, W.W. "Bob" and George Johnston, George Block, Sally LeBus, George LeBus, Mike Laverty, Russ & Kay Sylvester, Stan & Sandra Samuels, Ruth Bush, Alice Ewing, Bill Conley, Joe Haukebo, Kay Moore, Lil Sindel, Harold Geller, Billie (Burk) Wilkins Jack, Kathy Kalen, Connie Shelton

Online sources –

Vietnamveteransmemorial.org

Wikipedia.org

Chapter Nine: Black Lake

Publications —

Caperton, Thomas J., *Rogue,* Museum of New Mexico Press, Santa Fe

Julyan, Robert, *The Place Names of New Mexico,* University of New Mexico Press, Albuquerque

Sanchez, George I., *Forgotten People,* University of New Mexico Press, Albuquerque

Shuter, Marion, "The Elusive Roots of Black Lake," paper prepared for the History Department, New Mexico Highlands University, Las Vegas, New Mexico

Interview —

Ben Martinez

Index

Armijo, Governor Manuel 13
Axtell, Governor Samuel 21
AZL 81, 125-126, 128
Aztec Mine 55

B

Baca Grande 81, 125-126, 128, 133, 135, 138
Baca Grande Life 81
Baldy Mountain 15, 36-37, 52,-56, 76
  tunnel through 52
Baldy Town 42, 55, 173, 178
Balloons Over Angel Fire 148
Bankruptcy of Angel Fire Corporation 130
Barker, Elliott 145
Bartering among Native American tribes 30
Base lodge at Angel Fire ski area 125, 143
Beaubien, Charles 13-14
Beaubien-Miranda Land Grant 37, 122
Bergmann, Col. Edward 37
Big Ditch 41, 47, 52
Black Lake 152, 160
  and the Homestead Act 154, 156
  first survey of 157
  Indian trading route 30
Blades family 168, 183-189
Blades, Jim 183-189
Blue Lake 30, 33, 66, 79
Bobcat Pass 87
Bosque Redondo 16, 48
Boundaries determined by visual landmarks 13, 154
Bronson, Larry 35
Buffalo herds 30
Bull family 180-181
Bullington family 123, 130-131
Burk family 130-131, 161, 204
Buruel, Henry 125

C

Caddoan tribes 31
Calhoun, H.J., Sheriff of E'Town 44
Camp Elliott Barker 131, 145

F

G

H

I

M

Neal family 77, 130
Neal, Talmage (Tal) 54, 79, 82
Neal, T.D. 95-96
Neal, T.D. Store 75, 77, 177
Necas family 66
Newman, Simeon H. 19
New Mexico Geological Society 28
Nine Mile Creek 45
North American Continental Plate 27
The Northern New Mexico Miner 51
North Wind (lodge) 125

O

O'Neill, William 37
O'Neil, Pony 44
Orchard Realty 136
Ore smelting 69
Oro Dredging Company 52
Osha *(See Black Lake)*
Osha Mountain 152
Osha Pass 152

P

Palen, Judge Joseph 19
Palo Flechado Pass 27, 30, 45, 90, 125
  improved for autos 159
Payroll Mines 69
Pearson, John 50
Pearson's Saloon 45
Pecos, as a trading center 30
Pecos Pueblo 30
Pennsylvanian age 27
Philmont Scout Ranch 28, 55, 201
Picuris Pueblo, as a trading center 30
Piedmont-type plain 27
The Place Names of New Mexico 157
Placer claims 37-38
Plains Indians 29
Plante, Gary 129
Plaza Hotel 143
Pobar family 93-94

Did you enjoy this book?
Share the magic of the Moreno Valley
with friends and family!

Additional copies may be purchased through Moreno Valley businesses, museums, and visitor centers, and are available at most of the major online retailers.

MORE VINTAGE PHOTOS,
COURTESY OF OUR MORENO
VALLEY PIONEERS.

ENJOY!

Pete Andreoli - 1940's

Sam & Elliot Andreoli - ~1928

Horse-Drawn Wagon - 1952

Haystacks - 1946

Made in the USA
Monee, IL
16 November 2021